DOLLARS AND DEADLINES:

Make Money Selling Articles to Print and Online Markets

By Kelly James-Enger,
author of *Six-Figure Freelancing*

IMPROVISE PRESS

Copyright © 2013 by Kelly James-Enger
All rights reserved. No part of this book may be reproduced in any form or by any means, electronic or mechanical, including photocopying, recording, or by any information storage and retrieval system, without the written permission of the publisher. Published in the United States by Improvise Press.
Visit the Improvise Press Website: www.improvisepress.com
Printed in the United States of America
ISBN: 978-0-9836633-6-2

To the unpublished writers who want to become published—and paid

TABLE OF CONTENTS

Introduction	5
Chapter 1 Why Not Make Money Doing Something You Love?	7
Chapter 2 So What the Heck Do I Write About, Anyway?	10
Chapter 3 The Pitching Process: How to Approach Paying Markets	20
Chapter 4 There's More to Writing for Money than Writing	31
Chapter 5 Get a Contract Clue: What Every Writer Should Know	39
Chapter 6 Straight Talk about Money—and Taxes	52
Chapter 7 The Process, Demystified: How to Pitch, Research, and Write Short Articles	59
Chapter 8 Up the Ante: Tackling Longer Articles	88
Chapter 9 Expand your Repertoire: Writing Other Types of Articles	121
Chapter 10 Build your Freelance Arsenal with the 10 Essential Templates	147
Chapter 11 When the Worst Happens: 15 Freelance Crises and How to Handle Them	159

Chapter 12   165
What's Next? Expanding your Writing Career

Appendix   174

Index   176

INTRODUCTION

I've been writing for a living for nearly 16 years. And I've been writing *about* writing and freelancing for almost as long.

There are millions of writers out there. This book is not for all of them. It's for the writers who want to learn how to pitch, research, and write short nonfiction pieces—the articles that make up the majority of content for print and online markets.

If you're interested in writing for money, you may have heard my name before. I've authored other books for self-employed writers, including *Six-Figure Freelancing: The Writer's Guide to Making More Money* and *Writer for Hire: 101 Secrets to Freelance Success*. However, most of my work has been aimed at experienced writers who are already freelancing, and want to take their careers to the next level.

This book isn't for experienced writers. It's for the newbies. The writers who are just starting out. The writers without a clue.

You've never been published? No problem. You have no idea where to begin? No problem. If you want to write articles, and get paid for them, this is the book for you. It's based on the skills I've taught to hundreds of new writers—just like you—who sought to take the step from unpublished to published, and to be paid for their work in the process.

Follow the strategies and techniques in these pages, and you will learn how to write for money. You *will* get published, and you will get paid for your work. That may be a big promise for me to make, but I'm confident *you* can make it come true.

CHAPTER 1
Why Not Make Money Doing Something You Love?

So you like to write. Maybe you *love* to write. Lucky you!

But there's something even more satisfying than that—getting paid to do it.

And that's what this book will help you do.

It doesn't matter if you've never been published before.

It doesn't matter if you lack a college degree, or a high school diploma.

It doesn't matter whether you're a man or a woman, a teenager or a senior, a stay-at-home mom or a wage slave, a meaningless cog in a corporate wheel or a happy business owner.

What matters is that you write. You're writing already, or you have in the past. You know you can write. And you want to get paid to do it.

Sounds simple, right? So why aren't more of the millions of writers launching freelance careers, and getting paid for their words?

Those writers may not lack ability, or talent, or even drive. But they don't know how to take the first steps to launch successful careers. Because they don't know how to sell an article to a print or online market, which is how most serious, and well-paid, freelancers get started.

I'm not talking about writing. I'm talking about **writing for money**. (You're going to hear that phrase a lot in this book.)

If you don't care about making money for your writing, this isn't the book for you. Maybe you don't want to cheapen your ideals by having to please someone other than yourself, or you think that a true *artiste* shouldn't even have money on her radar. If so, more power to you.

But to me, there's a distinction between simply writing and getting paid to do it. To do the first, all you need is a minute or two (or more) and a way to record your words. To do the latter, you need more than that. Whether you want to ditch your day job and freelance fulltime or you want to make extra money to help support your family or you crave the satisfaction of getting paid to do something you love, being paid for your words takes you to another level as a writer.

I've been a fulltime freelance writer/author/ghostwriter since January, 1997. Since then I've written five books and hundreds of articles for print and online markets on successful freelancing. Through my books, blog, classes, and presentations, I've helped at least twelve hundred new writers transition from "newbies" to "published and paid." And that is an awesome transition, whether you get paid $500 or $50 or even $5 for your first piece.

It feels good to get paid to do something. It can legitimize your passion or be the first step of turning a hobby into a source of income.

Ten years ago, when I wrote the first edition of *Six-Figure Freelancing: The Writer's Guide to Making More Money*, I assumed my readers were already freelancing and were looking for ways to work more efficiently to increase their income. When I started my "Dollars and Deadlines" blog in May, 2010, though, I realized there were millions of writers I'd forgotten about. The writers who wanted to make a transition to published and paid but didn't know how. These writers didn't know how to improve their queries—they didn't even know what a query was! They'd never seen a freelance contract, much less tried to negotiate one. They lacked confidence when it came to sending their work out. They needed to know how to get started, regardless of what their end goals might be.

So I decided that my next freelancing book would be aimed at the writers who wanted to make that transition. The writers I'd forgotten about it. You're reading it now.

Yes, you have to be able to write, and write well, to make money as a writer. I won't teach you that in the pages that follow. What I will show you are the attributes you need as a successful freelance writer of nonfiction articles. (I use the word "article," "story," and "piece" throughout this book.) You'll learn what skills you must have, why they're so important, and how to strengthen them (or develop them if you don't have them already). I promise this book will give you a leg up on the millions of "would-be" and "wanna-be" writers. Unlike them, you'll have the essential tools you need to launch your freelance writing career. What you do with those tools is up to you!

A Note about Money

Before we move forward, though, I want to talk about money. Because this book isn't about writing—it's about writing for money. Yet there's a misconception that writers (other than a few household names) can't make money. I admit that are many writers who make very little from their work. But there are plenty who make a good living, and support themselves and their families, as fulltime freelancers. I personally know several hundred writers who make a good living selling nothing but their words, and I've done the same for 15+ years.

Want proof? Every year I conduct an income survey of fulltime freelancers. The 2012 survey asked 172 fulltime freelancers what they'd grossed in 2011, and what types of work they were doing. Out of those who responded:

16.96 percent made less than $20,000;
22.81 percent made between $20,000 and $39,999;
16.37 percent made between $40,000 and $59,999 (including me);
15.79 percent made between $60,000 and $79,999;

12.87 percent made between $80,000 and $99,999; and

15.20 percent broke the six-figure mark, making more than $100,000.

Breaking those numbers down, more than **one-quarter (28 percent) of full-time freelancers made more than $80,000 in 2012**, and a **full 43 percent made more than $60,000**. So don't buy into the myth that all freelancers are writing for peanuts. And many of these wealthy freelancers started out writing articles, and continue to write for print and online markets today.

Obviously the amount of money you make will depend on the type of work you produce, how much work you sell, and how much you get paid. But I want you to launch your career with the belief that you *can* make money with your words. Maybe even a lot of money.

So let's get started!

CHAPTER 2
So What the Heck Do I Write About, Anyway?

When you write for yourself, it's easy. You write what you want, when you want, for as long as you want. It's all about you. To make the transition to published and paid, though, you have to think about the market you're writing for, and specifically the editor who will pay you.

Sounds simple, right? But where do you start? By figuring out what you want to write, what you can write, and what types of markets you can write for.

As a newbie freelancer with no "clips" (published work) or experience, you should start out by pitching ideas that you have experience with. That experience can help you get your first few assignments; after you have some clips, or published articles, under your belt, you can expand to writing about other topics.

I guarantee that you already are an "expert" of sorts in a variety of subject areas. Your age, your gender, your livelihood, your background, your life experience, your hobbies, your locale, your interests—all of these things not only make you the person you are, but they're also possible topics to break into freelancing with.

I've taught freelancing classes and workshops for more than a decade and I always have my students start out by listing some of the subjects they have more than a passing knowledge of. They often start out worried that they won't be able to come up with any story ideas, but once they begin mining their lives, they find that they have plenty of subjects they can write about. The next question is finding markets, which we'll talk about in a bit.

A Real-Life Example: Me

When I started freelancing, I had no experience, no connections, and no clue. I didn't have a journalism degree, and everything I knew about freelancing I'd learned from reading books like *Writer's Market*. But I hadn't been living under a rock for thirty years. I'd had a life—at least something of one. I'd graduated from college and law school. I'd worked as a lawyer for more than five years. I'd experienced a "starter marriage." I'd gained 45 pounds (yikes!) my freshman year of college, and then lost the weight and kept it off. I'd flirted with vegetarianism and then committed to it in my late 20s. I was a child of divorce who'd grown up in a blended family. I'd been a runner for more than a decade.

I could go on and on, but here's my point: Nearly all of my first assignments as a new freelancer were topics I had some experience with. In my first book, *Ready, Aim, Specialize! Create your own Writing Specialty and Make More Money*, I listed some of those first articles and how I used my life experience, not my freelance experience (I didn't have any, remember?), to get assignments.

As a young, unhappy lawyer, I changed jobs four times in five years. That experience led to my first freelance sale—a piece on surviving your last two weeks on the job—to *Cosmopolitan*. My next sale was a story on avoiding legal problems as you plan your wedding. At the time I pitched it, I was planning my second wedding—and I was a lawyer, remember? That piece sold to *Bride's*.

Other sales followed, and I realized that while I was sending out dozens of queries, the pitches that were getting assigned all had something in common. The personal experience I had with the subject matter seemed to make up for my lack of actual writing experience. Here's how I used my background to garner some of those assignments:

- My husband and I were both in our late 20s when we met, and each had our own apartments. When we moved in together (I relocated to live with him), we had some disagreements about whose furniture should go where, how we'd decorate, and what we'd keep and what we'd get rid of. With the average age of newlyweds continuing to rise, I figured this topic—combining two households—would be a great topic for a bridal magazine. I sold the piece to *Bride's*.

- Remember how I'd toyed with vegetarianism? That's why a story in the local paper on a new vegetarian group caught my idea. I happened to know the founder of the group through a businesswomen's group I was a member of, and pitched a piece on how to create your own local vegetarian group (this was long before Facebook and other social media) to *Vegetarian Times* and it sold. My editor was so happy with my work that she assigned several other stories to me afterwards.

- I'd met my husband through a "fix-up," and while we clicked immediately, it was a case of opposites attracting. I'm a natural extrovert; Erik, not so much. Yet after years of dating fellow extroverts (who are great, really!), I found that my perfect mate was on the introverted side. That led to a pitch for a story titled, "When Opposites Attract," which sold to *For the Bride*. The story gave advice to newlyweds on how to recognize and appreciate each other's differences, and was the beginning of a decade-long relationship with the magazine.

- My pastor was training for RAGBRAI, or the Register's Annual Great Race Across Iowa, and using the event to raise money for charity. I pitched a piece about him for the religion section of the local newspaper, which assigned it. The story only paid $75, but it was a fun profile to write and helped me get other work from the features editor at the paper.

Get the idea? So start thinking about the topics and areas you already have a background in and can pitch to get your first few assignments. Once you gain experience, you have a good shot of getting other work, but starting out it makes a huge difference to pitch ideas you're what I call "uniquely qualified" to write.

Trust me, you already know more than the average person about a variety of subjects. Take your employment history. When I first started freelancing, I'd already worked at a variety of jobs. I'd done everything from practice law to deliver pizzas to lifeguard. I'd sold donuts and filed dental insurance claims. I even served drinks at a country western bar, where I briefly dated a fiddler named Jesse. But I digress.

No, I couldn't sell an idea based solely on my experience politely telling a 60-something geezer to get his hand off my butt, pronto, or on running a snack bar during "adult swim time," when hungry children swarmed the window waving their parents' $20 bills. If I pitched a piece on say, how to handle sticky work situations or discipline children that didn't belong to you, I'd still have to plan on doing additional research and conducting interviews with experts and real people. (More about that later.) But I *could* use my unique background to get my foot in the door as a new writer.

Your Life: A Font of Ideas

So think about your life, and start making a list of all of the subjects you could write about. Don't stop with your own experiences. Think too about people you know and/or have access to, like I did with my pastor. Your friends, your family, your neighbors, your coworkers—they're more than people you know. They're potential article ideas!

Even today, I continue to pitch ideas based on my own life or the experiences people around me are having. Often it's just a matter of finding the right market for that idea.

Start by listing possible ideas here:

_____

_____

_____

_____

_____

There are two basic ways to go about pitching an idea. One is to come up with an idea first, and then try to find a potential market for it. That's what I *used* to recommend for new writers. The second method is to find a market that you want to write for, and then come up with potential ideas for it.

Today, I suggest that writers use the second method. Here's why. Marketing, especially when you're a new freelancer, takes a huge amount of time. If you can find a market that you can write for multiple times, you cut your marketing time. It's much easier to sell an idea to an editor you've worked with before than to someone completely new.

I learned this lesson the hard way. I was so focused on coming up with saleable ideas as a new freelancer that I wound up doing a lot of "one-shots," where I would write about one subject for one market and then move on. So, I wrote one story on a charity car show for *The Lion* magazine, and then moved on. I wrote a profile for a magazine called *Accent on Living*, and moved on. I wrote a story for *Editor & Publisher,* and moved on. I sold a piece to a (now defunct) health website…and moved on.

You're getting the idea, right? Each of those stories took a lot of time to pitch, plus I had to research and write them afterwards. By never writing for those markets again, I wasted my time.

My career took off when I started to focus on markets that reflected more of my interests. For example, when I started freelancing fulltime, I was planning my wedding. Then, and as a newlywed, I had lots of bridal-related ideas. Well, I didn't write just one story for *Bridal Guide*. Because I came up with more ideas, I got more assignments. And then my editor started approaching me to assign ideas she'd come up with for me.

When I sold a piece to *For the Bride*, another national market, the same thing happened. Yes, I was still pitching, but now I was a known entity to my editor, and she responded more quickly than she would have to a complete stranger—and also reached out to assign ideas she had come up with to me.

So forget about selling one idea to one market. Start with markets you can write for more than once, and work with the goal of writing for that publication multiple times. That tip alone will make you more efficient (and smarter!) from the start.

Where Will You Sell Your Work?

As a freelancer, you sell your words for money. So let's switch gears and start talking about the types of potential markets you may write for:

Online Markets

What they are: Way back, when, when I started freelancing, I wrote almost exclusively for print magazines. Online magazines were in their infancy, but today most freelancers who write articles do so for a mix of print and online publications. There are tens of thousands of websites and online publications that hire freelancers, so it's not surprising that according to my annual freelance income survey, three out of four freelancers made money writing for the Web in 2011. This includes writing for Websites as well as creating the content that is published in electronic magazines, or "e-zines."

What they pay: Rates for online sites vary widely, but "good" online markets pay about $0.25 to $1-2/word for articles. Larger, more established websites tend to pay higher rates, and stories that require more research tend to pay higher rates. If it's unclear from the website what its rates are, don't hesitate to send an email to request that information, or ask a writer who's worked for the market.

Where to find markets/clients: First, look for the online versions of your favorite print magazines. Nearly all of them have their writers' guidelines listed somewhere on the site. You'll find online writing gigs listed at websites including:

- www.gorkanajobs.com;
- www.journalismjobs.com;
- www.online-writing-jobs.com;
- www.freelancewritinggigs.com; and
- www.mediabistro.com.

The above Websites are all free, but there are fee-based sites that provide online market information as well:

- www.freelancesuccess.com. This online weekly newsletter includes a market guide and access to an online community of subscribers for networking. $99/year.
- www.freelanceswitch.com. This site includes online job postings aimed at both web developers and writers; $7/month.
- www.writers-editors.com. This site includes free content, but for $29/year you also receive a monthly newsletter full of markets, many of which are online.

How to break in: As with any kind of market, you want to demonstrate that you're familiar with the publication that you're querying, and pitch an idea that is right for the market. Use a query letter that catches the editor's attention, shows why readers will be interested, explains how you'll approach the topic, and shows that you're uniquely qualified to write the piece.

Online articles tend to be shorter than those in print publications and often include interactive elements like quizzes. If you have any doubts about what to write, follow the format of other articles already published on the site. In fact, following the format is always good advice regardless of what type of publications you're writing for.

Blogs

What they are: Blogs are a specialized online market, and one of the easiest for new writers to break into, especially if you already maintain your own blog. Nearly half of freelancers made money from blogging in 2011.

What they pay: Short answer? It depends on the blog. Rather than paying per-word, most blogs pay a set amount per blog post, which can be as little as $10 or $20 to $250 and up. Established blog writers say that a typical rate (for a blog post of 500 to 800 words) ranges from $50 to $500. While blog rates are sometimes lower than other online publications, many freelancers find that they can write for the same blog over and over, making for steady work with little pitching time.

Where to find markets/clients: You may already be following some blogs you want to write for. To find more markets, use Google to search for blogs in the subject area you write about. Check the blog's guidelines to see if its owner accepts posts, and whether (and what) it pays.

How to break in: To break into blogging for money, first check the guidelines for submitting work. Many blogs prefer to see the blog post itself instead of sending a formal query letter. If you do query, highlight your knowledge of the blog's subject area, and your own blogging experience to get an assignment.

Print Markets

Consumer Magazines

What they are: Consumer magazines are what most of us think of when we think of writing for magazines. *Sports Illustrated. Time. Parents. Better Homes and Gardens. The New Yorker. Fitness. Cosmopolitan.* Consumer mags are the publications that you'll find on a newsstand, at a supermarket, or at a bookstore. They may have the entire country as their audience ("national" magazines) or be a local or regional publication which is aimed at a smaller geographic area. Two-thirds of the freelancers surveyed write for them.

What they pay: Typically it depends on the circulation, or circ, of the magazine. National magazines with big circulations tend to start at $1-2/word; smaller circ publications pay less, down to about $0.10/word. Regional consumer magazines have lower rates, in the $0.10-0.50/word range.

Where to find markets/clients: Start with the magazines you're already familiar with—I've always had the most success pitching publications I know inside and out. Create a list of possible markets by using market guides like *Writer's Market*, and check their Websites for their writers' guidelines.

How to break in: Consumer print magazines pay more than any other type of periodical, so they're inundated with queries from both new and experienced freelancers. That's why I suggest new writers focus on breaking in by pitching a short article for the magazine's front-of-book ("FOB") section. An editor is more likely to give a new writer a chance with a shorter piece and once you've proven yourself, you can always pitch longer pieces.

You're facing a lot of competition, so make your query as strong as you can. Pitch an idea you have some kind of personal knowledge of (there's that **uniquely qualified** idea again—more about that in chapter 3), and let the editor know that you've read her publication by suggesting the section of the publication you think the piece belongs in.

If you're pitching a local or regional magazine, make sure that you include a local angle to whatever topic you're querying. If you don't get a response from the editor, send a follow-up letter, including the original query, and (politely) ask her for a response. If you still don't hear from the editor, move on to another publication you think may be interested in the idea.

Custom Magazines

What they are: A custom magazine is a hybrid of sorts. It *looks* like a consumer magazine but it's aimed at a very specific audience. For example, if you're a member of AAA, you get a magazine in the mail called *Home and Away*, which covers topics including local travel and car maintenance. If you're a member of LifeTime Fitness, you get a magazine called *Experience Life*, which is about healthy living. These magazines resemble consumer magazines but typically are "controlled circulation," meaning they're not available on newsstands. Half of freelancers surveyed write for them.

What they pay: Each publishing company that produces custom magazines sets the pay rate for its articles. I've seen rates as low as $0.25/word, but more commonly in the $0.50-$1/word range.

Where to find markets/clients: The Custom Content Council (www.customcontentcouncil.com) includes a list of custom content publishers. Also, ask friends and family to collect custom magazines for you, and check market guides like *The Standard Periodical Directory*. [See Trade Magazines, below.]

How to break in: You can send a query to a custom publication, but I've found sending a letter of introduction ("LOI"), to be more efficient. [See chapter 9 for an LOI template.] Rather than pitching a specific idea the way you do with a query, an LOI highlights your background and experience that is most likely to appeal to the editor of the market. (So, if you're pitching *Home and Away*, you'd want to include the fact that you travel 40,000 miles a year and have become something of a "B and B" expert in the process.

Trade Magazines

What they are: Trade magazines are aimed at people in a particular career, trade, or industry. If you own a restaurant, for example, you might subscribe to *Restaurants & Institutions Magazine, Food Industry News*, or *Chain Leader*. Nearly half of freelancers—46 percent—wrote for trades in 2011.

What they pay: Some trades don't pay for freelance material, but those that do pay lower rates than consumer magazines, usually in the $0.20-50/word range.

Where to find markets/clients: If you already have experience in a particular industry or business, start with the trade magazines you're familiar with. Otherwise, check your local library for Bacon's Magazine Directory, Gale Directory of Publications and Broadcast Media, or The Standard Periodical Directory, all of which list trade publications.

How to break in: The most efficient way to approach a trade magazine is with an LOI. Editors at trades usually know what ideas they'll be covering (and may have a specific editorial calendar to follow) but need writers who can research and write about those topics. When you query, make sure you play

LOI = letter of introduction

up any relevant knowledge you have of the industry to set yourself apart from other freelancers.

Newspapers

What they are: Newspapers aren't doing as well as they used to be, but they're not dead yet. Major newspapers like *The New York Times*, *The Wall Street Journal*, and *The Chicago Tribune* still acquire freelance work and pay for it, and there are more than 15,000 national, regional, and local newspapers in the United States today that have both print and online versions.

What they pay: It depends on the market. Some newspapers pay by the word, like magazines, while others, particularly smaller markets, pay a set amount—maybe $25-75 for a feature, depending on the market's size. Larger markets tend to pay by the word, at about $0.25-50/word and up, depending on the writer's experience and depth of reporting required.

Where to find markets/clients: Start with your local papers, and go from there. If you're aiming at national markets, look for them online, and make sure you check the guidelines before you pitch.

How to break in: Just as when pitching a magazine, you'll want to query your idea to the appropriate editor. (Check the newspaper's guidelines to determine who the right person to pitch is.) Your query letter should include a compelling lead; a "why write it" section that provides more detail about the idea and shows why readers will be interested in the piece; a "nuts and bolts" section that explains how you'll approach the topic (i.e. what types of sources will you interview? How long will the article be?); and what I call an ISG, or an "I'm-so-great" section where you highlight your relevant qualifications.

If you're pitching a local newspaper, I suggest that you offer to cover events (like school or county board meetings, for example) in your query. This can be a way to get your foot in the door with a local publication and lead to other assignments.

Locating Potential Markets

Okay. Now you know what types of markets you can write for. Under "online markets," I already gave you some of the many websites you can use to actually find them. Here are five more ways to locate publications you can sell to:

Use your legs. Even though there may be fewer brick-and-mortar bookstores out there, there are still thousands of stores that carry magazines. Independent bookstores and newsstands, big-box stores like Target and Wal-Mart, and even grocery stores have hundreds of magazines available. Why not make your weekly trip to the grocery store do double-duty and stock up on margarine *and* magazines. If you're too lazy to leave the house, check out the magazines on Amazon.com.

Hit the library. Yes, you've probably heard of *Writer's Market*, an annual volume of book and magazine publishers that comes out in late August every year. You may even have a copy. But chances are that you haven't heard of

ISG
I'm so great

several volumes that dwarf this popular book, which I mentioned in the trade markets section.

Ask your local reference librarian if your library carries any of the following books—they're quite expensive. Each is updated annually and contains tens of thousands of potential markets:

- *Bacon's Newspaper/Magazine Directory;*
- *Gale Directory of Publications and Broadcast Media;* and
- *Standard Periodical Directory.*

If your library doesn't keep copies on reserve (my library used to carry all three and now only maintains a copy of the *Standard Periodical Directory*), find out which library does. It's worth an afternoon to read through market possibilities (don't forget your laptop so you can take notes while you're there.) And make sure you ask if there are any databases you can use to search for markets. Librarians often have access to databases that patrons do not.

Chat up your friends. I'm always looking for markets and I ask my friends to keep magazines for me. They subscribe to or come across magazines I might not see otherwise. The more friends you have and the more varied their professions and hobbies, the better—ask them to keep all of their magazines for you tell them that you will be happy to recycle them when you're done.

Get on Google. In addition to the sites already listed, don't forget to use Google or another search engine to search for possible markets. For example, I find a lot of reprint markets by putting in phrases like "regional bridal magazine" or "local bridal magazine" and then checking out the sites that come up. Enter a keyword that relates to the subject of the publication you're looking for and add "magazine" or "publication" (or "online" if you're looking for web-based mags) for markets.

Stay healthy. Even a routine doctor's visit can turn into market research. Arrive early to check out the magazines—you're likely to find a slew of publications aimed at a wide variety of readers. I've found potential markets from everywhere from my pediatrician's office to the local urgent care center to the Y where I work out. Just make sure you ask permission from the receptionist before you slip the magazine into your briefcase or purse—or make some quick notes about editors' names and contact information before your name is called.

Identifying Potential Markets

As you come across markets you think you'd like to write for, write them down. Keep a running list of target publications, focusing on ones that you think you could write for more than once. List some of your initial targets here:

_____

_____

_____

_____

_____

_____

This is only your starting list of markets; you'll no doubt come across more as you continue to freelance. I suggest you choose two or three to focus on at the outset, and go from there.

The Next Step

At this point, you should have a running list of potential article ideas. That's **step one**.

Step two is identifying some potential markets for those ideas.

Step three is putting those two things together, and creating a query to sell your idea, and yourself, to your target market. In chapter 3, you'll learn how to do that.

CHAPTER 3
The Pitching Process: How to Approach Paying Markets

I'll tell you what separates writers who make no money and those who write and get paid for it. It's not talent, or inspiration, drive, or even luck. It's the willingness to sell themselves.

Freelancing is a competitive business. If you happen to be fortunate enough to have a relative, close friend, or former college roommate who hands you assignments, good for you! (And yes, I'm jealous.) If you're like the majority of us, though, you have to open your own doors, and make your own connections. And that's where pitching comes in.

Wanna-be writers don't get this. They may not even realize that you don't sit down, write an article, send it in, and pray to get published. (That's inefficient, first off, and brands you an amateur.)

Actually I do want to brand you. But I want to brand you as a pro. Someone who "gets" freelancing and understands how editors work and how they want to be approached. In this chapter, you'll learn how to write a query that will position you as a pro, and set you up for assignments—even if your first query is rejected. Just keep these three principles in mind when you contact a potential market:

1. Your editor is very busy.
2. Your editor wishes someone would make his or her life better. Or easier. Better yet, both.
3. **You** are that person!

That's it. I'm not joking. Every pitch you send should keep your editor's needs in mind; demonstrate how you (or your story idea) will help her; and make the case that **you** are the writer she needs, at least for this particular assignment.

How do you do that? With a killer query, or, in some instances, with a kick-ass LOI. [Remember you'll find an LOI in chapter 10.] But we'll focus on queries in this chapter, as they are still the primary way new freelancers nab assignments.

The Query, Demystified

You have an idea. Now it's time to write a query letter, or query. (But query's a verb, too. You can write a query, or you can query a publication. Both are legit uses of the word.) The query is the way you introduce yourself to an editor. This one-page letter is likely your only opportunity to make a positive first impression, capture her attention with an idea that will work for her readers, and convince her or him to give you your first assignment. It's important.

I've been using the same basic structure for queries for years, and I know it works. Each query includes four elements:

• The **lead.** This first paragraph or two should capture the reader's attention. You don't need to start your query with an introduction; instead, jump right into your story and write the lead of the article you intend to write. You may use a first-person or third-person anecdote; a recent research breakthrough; a surprising fact; or any other introduction that makes your editor keep reading.

• The **why-write-it** section. This paragraph gives more detail about the article you're pitching so that the editor can decide whether it's right for her readers.

• The **nuts-and-bolts** section. This paragraph describes how you'll approach the article. Who do you plan to interview? How long will the article be? What angle will you use? What's the working title? I always like to suggest the section of the publication I believe the story belongs here. It shows I'm familiar with the market I'm pitching, which helps set me apart from other writers.

• The **ISG** (for **"I'm-So-Great"**) paragraph. This is arguably the most important section of the query for an unpublished writer. You're unknown and unproven, so you want to demonstrate that you're the perfect person to write this particular story.

Before we get into some query examples, let me explain about "lead time." Lead time is the amount of time between when a publication assigns stories and when they actually run. Typically, national consumer magazines have the longest lead times—on average, about six months. Smaller magazines and trade publications tend to have shorter lead times, and online publications have the shortest, which may be only a week or two.

You want to think about lead time when you're pitching an idea that has some kind of "time peg," or reason to run the story at a particular time. For example, you'd probably pitch a holiday-themed story to a national woman's magazine in early summer, and a "get ready for the beach" workout for a spring issue of a men's fitness magazine in fall or early winter. The publication's writers' guidelines may tell you what its lead time is; if there's any doubt, it's always better to pitch a story a little early than too late.

In fact, I suggest you always review the market's writers' guidelines **before** you write a query. The guidelines may specify what editors like to see in pitches, and tell you which sections of the publication are written in-house or are otherwise unavailable to freelancers. The guidelines will also tell how to send your query (i.e., via email or regular mail) and may also give you a suggested response time.

Here's an example of a straightforward query using the above template. I've included my comments in brackets. (You'll see me use this technique—setting off my comments in brackets—throughout the book, when I want to draw attention to something in an example or template I'm sharing. These comments are for you, the reader. They were not included in anything I wrote or turned in! You'll also see me set off sections of contracts and templates to make them easier to recognize.)

Dear Jane:

Last month, I was in Madison, Wisconsin to teach a weeklong class. Madison's a great town to run in, and one gorgeous evening I headed out for an easy five-miler. The run was awesome—I felt well-oiled, relaxed, and unstoppable. Two blocks from my hotel, I picked up the pace. I was running hard as I sped down the slight decline of Langdon Street. I was flying! And then suddenly, I really was flying—literally.

I've tripped and fallen many times before (I'm a bit uncoordinated), but this time I fell so fast I couldn't get my hands up to catch myself. I broke my fall with my head. By the time I limped back to the hotel with a bloody, egg-sized lump on my forehead and a nasty case of road rash, my vision was blurring. At the emergency room, I learned I'd suffered a mild concussion. I was lucky—as the ER doc told me, it could have been much worse. [This is a first-person anecdotal lead. A first-person lead is a great way to start a pitch if you're a new writer as it shows you know something about the subject.]

Runners occasionally take spills that produce far worse than a scraped knee or a twisted ankle. In fact, seven million Americans a year seek treatment for sports-related injuries, more than one million of which involve the head or neck region. Head injuries are particularly troubling as they tend to be more severe than other sports-related injuries. Their effects can also last for months—even a seemingly mild bump can cause brain injury and lead to post-concussion syndrome, which includes symptoms like poor memory, headaches, dizziness, and irritability. [This paragraph reveals that I've done some homework on sports-related injuries. I cite recent statistics to prove how common they are, and how serious head injuries in particular can be. I think I've demonstrated why Jane's readers should care about this article as there's a good chance that they too will be injured at some point.]

My article, "Head First," will explain the risks and symptoms of head injuries and describe how to reduce the chance of experiencing one while running or doing other activities. (In my case, I had several factors working against me: I was running downhill, on a brick sidewalk, in fading evening light—all of which made me more likely to stumble.) I'll interview several respected physicians about the dangers of head injuries; a sidebar might include a list of the sports most likely to cause a head injury. While I estimate a length of 1,000 words, that's flexible depending on your needs. [I've included a working title, explained whom I plan to interview—though I could have given the name of a specific sports medicine or ER doc—and told her how many words my story will be. I've also suggested a possible sidebar.]

Interested in this story for your "Warm-ups" section? I'm a long-time runner (marathon best 3:26) who's been a fulltime freelancer for more than seven years; during that time, my health, nutrition and fitness articles have appeared in 50 national magazines including *Self, Shape, Health, Redbook, Woman's Day, Continental,* and *Marie Claire*; I'll be happy to send you clips via snail mail if you like. [I've suggested the section of the magazine the story fits in to let Jane know I'm familiar with her market. I've also mentioned that I'm a runner, which is relevant here. If I didn't already have clips, I would have written something like, "I believe my recent experience will help bring a unique perspective to this important topic." As a new writer, make sure you make the case for why *you* should write the article you're pitching.]

Jane, I hope you'll find this important topic appropriate for an upcoming issue of the new-and-improved *Runner's World*. Please let me know if you have any questions about it. [Typical closing language. This query led to my first piece for *Runner's World*, a story on avoiding and treating "on-the-run" injuries.]

Sincerely,
Kelly James-Enger

Here's another example of a straightforward, yet effective query:

Dear Kristin:

When I launched my fulltime freelance business on January 1, 1997, I did so without any help. I had no journalism background, no clients, no connections in the publishing world, and a portfolio that contained only two clips. I made every mistake possible along the way. I wrote articles and sent them to markets instead of sending queries. I took what editors offered without asking for more money. I signed all-rights contracts without negotiating to make them more writer-friendly. I wrote for markets once instead of trying to develop long-term relationships. The list goes on…and on…and on.

But over time, I started to learn from my mistakes. I looked for ways to work more efficiently. I focused on building relationships with editors, experts, and other writers. I cut back on the amount of time I spent researching stories, which boosted my bottom line. And I discovered ways to set myself apart from all the other writers out there clamoring for editors' attention. It paid off—along the way, I've written hundreds of articles, two novels, three nonfiction books, and hit the six-figure mark as a freelancer. [This is another first-person lead. Do you see how I'm catching the editor's attention with a "true-life" story **and** demonstrating that I'm uniquely positioned to write this article?]

Yet I see many writers making the same kinds of mistakes I did early on, which prevent them from reaching their monetary and personal goals. "The Biggest Mistakes Even Smart Writers Make" will describe these kinds of errors, how they affect your productivity, and show ways to overcome them. I'm thinking of breaking the article into five to eight sections (depending on how many mistakes you want me to cover), with practical, doable advice for each type of error. [This paragraph explains how I'll approach the story, and shows the editor how her readers will benefit from the piece. In retrospect, I could have included a couple of examples of these types of mistakes to further strengthen this section.]

Kristin, are you interested in this topic for your "Work Smarter" section? I estimate 1,500 words for this piece, but that's flexible depending on your needs. About me: I've been a fulltime freelancer for seven years, and wrote an article on reprints for *Writer's Digest* last year. My work has also appeared in more than 50 national magazines including *Self, Shape, Health, Redbook, Woman's Day, Continental, The Writer,* and *Marie Claire,* and I'm the author of four books including *Ready, Aim, Specialize! Create your own Writing Specialty and Make More Money* (The Writer Books, 2003) and the upcoming *Six-Figure Freelancing: The Writer's Guide to Making More Money* (Random House, February, 2005.) If you like, I'll be happy to send you clips via fax or snail mail. [Note that I've suggested the section of the magazine where I think the story belongs. I've also given her a word estimate that is consistent with the writers' guidelines, and told her a little bit about my background.]

Please let me know if you have any questions about this idea. I believe readers will appreciate and benefit from this story. [Oops! I forgot to thank her for her time. Otherwise, I think this is a great query, and it sold.]

Sincerely,
Kelly James-Enger

I want you to see that these queries are not complicated, yet make a good case for me being the writer to handle the piece. Let's look at another query. This was written back in 1996, when I was still a lawyer, and freelancing on the side. It was also sent via snail mail, which was the preferred method of contacting editors then:

Mr. Daniel Kehrer
Editor
Independent Business: American's Small Business Magazine
Group IV Communications, Inc.
125 Auburn Court #100
Thousand Oaks, CA 91362-3617

Dear Mr. Kehrer:

The fastest growing area of civil lawsuits is employment law. More disgruntled employees and job applicants are filing discrimination charges and lawsuits than ever before—and it's not just large companies that get sued. Small businesses may not have liability insurance to cover these types of claims and the legal fees involved in defending them can be astronomical. How do small business owners *avoid* claims of employment discrimination—and how can they protect themselves in the event of a bogus claim? [Oh my goodness. As I read this, I'm cringing at my lack of experience. A quick visit to the Equal Employment Opportunity Commission—the EEOC—would have given me hard stats to back up my claim that more discrimination claims are being filed than ever before. But I was a new writer, remember? I didn't realize I needed to demonstrate my ability to do research as part of the query-writing process. That being said, I don't think this lead is terrible. It's definitely an attention-getter if you're a small business owner, the target audience of this business publication. Another option would be to have interviewed a small business owner who had recently defended a discrimination claim and used a third-person anecdote as a lead.]

This is the topic I am interested in exploring for *Independent Business*. As an attorney who concentrates in defending businesses in labor and employment matters and a freelance writer, I am **uniquely qualified** [my emphasis] to cover this subject for your magazine. I envision a brief overview of the discrimination laws, noting which ones apply to small businesses, suggestions on how to interview job applicants without asking illegal questions, and ways to discipline and terminate employees with less risk of being sued. [I was thinking "uniquely qualified" before I started freelancing fulltime, and I think I've done a good job of demonstrating that I am well-positioned to write on this subject. But do you see how broad the story is I'm pitching? I'd be better off focusing on one aspect of this subject instead of trying to cover so much. Note that I haven't told the editor how many words I envision, or suggested a section of the magazine for this piece. I also haven't said who I plan to interview for the piece. Overall, this section is pretty weak for those reasons.]

I have enclosed a copy of my resume and a piece I recently sold to *Bride's* magazine to give you an idea of my writing style—when writing for non-lawyers, I am careful to stay away from legal jargon. I hope you will find that this idea will be a timely addition to an upcoming issue of either magazine, and I look forward to hearing from you soon. [Okay, this is so amateurish! Why am I enclosing my resume? Freelancers don't do that unless an editor requests it. And I shouldn't have enclosed my *Bride's* article—it hadn't even been published yet! My intentions are good, but this paragraph definitely brands me as a rookie. I cringe at it now. And yet, a year later, when I finally followed up on it, the editor asked me to write the piece—though with a *very* detailed assignment letter that specified everything from word count to the number and types of sources (i.e. business attorneys and small business owners from throughout the country) I had to interview to how many sections the piece should include. I realize now he knew I was new to freelancing and needed handholding and direction. The good news is that I did a great job on the piece, and it was my first big feature.]

Thank you for your time and consideration.

Very truly yours,
Kelly K. James

Use these queries as templates for your own, keeping the four basic parts in mind. And remember while an article's purpose may be to inform, educate, entertain, or provoke (or all four), a query's primary purpose is to sell. You hope to have the right idea to the right editor at the right publication at the right time. But a well-written query can open the door to a publication, even if the editor isn't interested in the specific idea you pitched. I've had editors offer me other assignments based on my query-writing skills, because they know if you can research and write a compelling query, you can tackle an article as well.

Think Small, at Least at First

There's something else to keep in mind when you're trying to get your first freelance assignment. As a novice (and unproven) writer, you're far more likely to get a shorter piece assigned than a longer one.

First, a shorter piece is easier to research and write. Second, if you fail to deliver your assignment or you turn in something unusable (you're an unproven writer, remember? Your editor is taking a chance on you!), your editor only has a small hole to fill on the page. And most established freelancers don't bother with short pieces, so you're facing less competition than if you're pitching a longer article. Look at the front of the magazine (the FOB section) for departments that use shorter articles of up to 500 words or so. I've found that online markets and blogs also tend to be more open to new writers, possibly because they usually need more content than their print counterparts.

How do you know which editor to pitch? Start with the magazine's website, and if the information isn't provided there, call or email the magazine. I've found that a quick phone call is the fastest way to learn the name of the appropriate editor. Most publications prefer email queries, but a few still like to receive them by snail mail. Follow the publication's guidelines in terms of how you submit your query.

Before you send your query, read it over and ask yourself whether you've written a compelling lead, given her enough detail about the subject, explained how you plan to approach the story, and demonstrated both your knowledge of the subject and of the market you're pitching. If not, rework your query until you're satisfied with it.

Finally, make sure you proofread your query letter! It's likely the only opportunity to make a positive first impression with the editor you're contacting. Don't let a typo or misspelling sink you.

That's it. Hit "send" on your query, unless it's one of the few publications that prefer to be contacted by regular mail and congratulate yourself for getting your pitch out.

As a new freelancer, the majority of your pitches are likely to be query letters. As you gain experience, though, you may start adding an LOI to your marketing repertoire. Starting out, though, expect to spend the majority of your time coming up with ideas and writing pitches. It's part of the process.

No Response? Follow Up

Often a publication's guidelines will tell you when to expect a response. If they do not, or if you haven't heard from the editor in eight to twelve weeks, send a polite follow-up email. I use language like the following:

Dear Stephanie:

Hope you're doing well. I'm writing to follow up on a query I sent you (working title, "Sleep Yourself Thin") four weeks ago; I've dropped it below for your convenience. [Remind the editor of your pitch, and include it in your follow-up (in the body of the email, not as an attachment) to make it easy for her.]

Would you let me know at your earliest opportunity if you're interested in this story for *Complete Woman*? If I don't hear from you within two weeks, I'll assume you're not interested in the idea at this time and may market it elsewhere. [With a follow-up, you put the onus on the *editor* to get back to *you*. If she wants the piece, great! If not, I'm not going to sit around for months hoping for a response. I've found that following up tends to provoke a response—even if it's "thanks, but no thanks." You can give a market more time to respond--say three to four weeks--if you like. The idea is to give the editor (and yourself) a deadline.]

Thank you very much for your time; I look forward to hearing from you soon. [Standard closing line.]

Very truly yours,
Kelly James-Enger

If your target market turns you down, or if you don't hear back within the deadline you gave the editor, choose another market for your idea, and get the query out to that publication. Just because one editor says "no" doesn't mean another won't say "yes!" Just make sure that you tweak your query, if necessary, to match the needs of the new potential market.

When I have a good idea, I shop it around until I sell it—or until I run out of markets to approach! I'm not joking. I had one idea that was rejected by nine markets. But the tenth one bought it. Had I given up at any point along the way, I wouldn't have made that sale. So don't let rejection derail you.

In fact, one of the best tips I can give you about pitching is to **expect rejection.** You *will* get rejected. I guarantee it! So stop worrying about it. Have a plan for what you will do when you get rejected. My personal rule of thumb is what I call the **24-hour rule.** That means that when I get a rejection (and I have received more than 1,000 of them at this point!), I do two things within 24 hours.

First, I get the query out to a new market. I call this a "resubmission," or a resub. *Woman's Day* didn't want the idea? No problem. I'd try *Family Circle*. *Parents* said no? Then I tried *Parenting* instead. If *The Chicago Tribune* rejected me, I'd try the *Chicago Sun-Times*. A pitch isn't doing you any good sitting on your hard drive. As soon as you get a no, or you don't receive a response, you need to get that query out to another place.

Second, and this may seem counterintuitive, I'd come up with a new pitch for the editor who had turned me down. I'd start this query by saying something like, "Thank you for your response [note that I don't say rejection!] to my query about perfectionism. I'm sorry you can't use the idea right now, but I have another query I'd love for you to consider." Then I would start my new query.

There were some instances where even multiple queries produced nothing more than a series of rejections. After a half-dozen of those, yes, it's time to move on. But with many other markets, it wasn't my first query that got me an assignment. It was my second, or third, or fourth. I didn't give up, and eventually I got that assignment, and started writing for that market!

Yet most new writers get a rejection and never query that market again. Don't be that writer! Give yourself a tight deadline—I like 24 hours but you can choose a timeframe that works for you—and get a new query out to your original publication and resub your initial idea to another market within that amount of time. You'll turn what was a rejection into two opportunities and boost your chances of succeeding as a freelancer.

Reslant Whenever You Can

There's another simple way to boost your query effectiveness. Try to "reslant" every idea and send it out to more than one market at a time.

Here's what I mean. Let's take the original query from this chapter, when I pitched the idea of how to avoid head injuries—and what to do if you experience one—to *Runner's World*. That's one idea that I sent to one market. But I could have easily pitched a similar idea to another market. I could have tweaked the idea to focus on head injuries and concussions in kids (a big issue right now especially among youth and adult football players) to a parenting or women's magazine. I could have pitched the same idea to an online health or fitness market, or focused on the fact that seniors are more likely to experience a head injury and tweaked it for a 50+ print or online magazine. I could have broadened the idea a bit and pitched a piece on avoiding fitness-related injuries to a fitness magazine like *Men's Health* or *Self*. There are an almost infinite number of ways I can reslant the initial idea for other markets.

Get the idea? I do have one rule I follow when I reslant, though—**I do not pitch a competing market with the same idea at the same time**. The reason is simple. I'm trying to build relationships with editors. If I pitch the same idea to competing pubs (think *Details* and *Men's Health*), and editors at both magazines decide they love the idea and want to assign it, they will not be happy to discover I'm writing or going to write about it for their biggest competitor!

So reslant away. Just be sure that you're reslanting to markets that don't compete with one another for readers—at least not at the same time.

Track your Progress and Set Goals

As you're sending out queries, make sure you keep track of them. Keep a running list of the queries you've sent out to which markets, follow-ups, and their status. Over time, you should notice that you get fewer "nos" and more assignments. That's evidence that your queries are getting stronger, and that you're becoming "known" to editors. Both of those are good things.

I'll make another suggestion as you're starting out, too. Set some goals for yourself, even if they're small ones. You've probably heard of "SMART" goals, which stands for Specific, Measureable, Attainable, Realistic, and Time-based. A SMART goal for you might be to send out one query/week, or to spend three hours every weekend researching potential markets. Or you might set a certain number of queries to send out every month, or that you'll follow up on every pitch within a certain time period. My 24-hour rule is an example of a SMART goal, and one that works. I don't have to worry about what I'll do when I receive a bong. I use my SMART goal to resub that query to another market, and send a new query to the editor at the original publication.

It's fine to have a goal of making, say, $20,000 a year from your freelance income, or to write for national magazines, or to make enough money to quit your day job. Just keep in mind that it's the SMART goals—the small but specific steps you take—that will help you achieve your larger ones.

A Super Awesome Bonus (If You Need It)

Don't despair if it takes you far longer than you expected to write your first few queries. Crafting a solid query is a skill and one that takes some time to develop. As you gain experience, you'll find that you're able to envision and produce your queries more quickly.

Still worried about a particular query? Can't make yourself hit "send?" I'll make you this offer. Email it to me at dollarsanddeadlines@gmail.com with "super awesome bonus" in the subject line and I will look it over for you. Give me a day or two to send it back, and you'll feel more confident about the content and format of your query. I can't promise that your query will be accepted and assigned, but I can assure you that your query won't have major problems that will peg you as an amateur.

Let me add one thing before we move on. You may notice I haven't discussed whether you need a blog, or a website, or a Twitter handle, or a special Facebook page for your writing as you start out. There's a good reason why. You **don't**.

Let me clarify. Yes, as you gain experience, sure, it's nice to have a website where you can showcase samples of your work. And you may want to follow some of your editors and/or markets on Twitter. Maybe you're already blogging, and your pitch is related to the subject of your blog. That's all great.

But do you **need** a website, or a blog, or 10,000 followers on Twitter, or anything else social-media related to launch your freelance career? Nope. What you do need are ideas, markets to pitch to, and query letters—which you should be working on at this point. I'd rather see you spend your time focusing on your killer queries than worrying about your social media presence of what color your Website should be. As you gain clips and experience, you can get your own site up or create a LinkedIn page. For now, let's focus on the pitching, which is what gets you assignments.

CHAPTER 4
There's More to Writing for Money than Writing

You've sent out your first query or two. Good for you! But before we move into the basics of researching and writing articles for publications, let's talk about some emotional aspects of writing for money that some books on the subject ignore.

Number one, sometimes writing for money—especially when you write for a living—sucks. I'm not kidding. Writing has been my chosen profession for nearly sixteen years, but I don't enjoy writing every day. Some days I hate it. But just like Dorothy Parker said, while I sometimes hate to write, I love **having written**.

When I speak to writers in person, I explain the discrepancy by talking about the difference between wanting to *go* to the gym and wanting to *have gone* to the gym. Students get it immediately, laughing and nodding in recognition.

So, when someone tells me he wants to write a book (and this happens a lot!), I think to myself, "No, he doesn't. He wants to **have written** a book." Most of us are lazy by nature. We want the big pay-off, the Lotto jackpot of the finished manuscript, the satisfaction of reaching our goal without all that piddling, time-consuming, draining work.

But it doesn't happen like that. You can't reach the prize of publication and being paid without putting in the labor along the way. And that means writing. Not thinking about writing, not dreaming about writing, not fantasizing about writing, not reading about writing … writing.

Yes, you have to research markets. Yes, you have to develop ideas. And reading good writing can help your own. As long as you actually, you know, write. So reading this book (and recommending it to your friends) is a great start to get you writing for money. But it's only the beginning. The rest is up to you.

Strive for PMA

You pour yourself a glass of chardonnay, and drink half. Is the glass now half-full or half-empty? The answer depends on whether you're an optimist or a pessimist (and on how much you enjoy chardonnay).

Which are you? Do you naturally tend to look at the upside of things or do you live in the doldrums? I often tell my overly melodramatic seven-year-old, "Your attitude makes a difference. You can decide whether you want to have fun—or not."

Not that freelancing, or even writing, is fun every single day. People who say that are either lying, deluded, or way more Pollyanna-ish than I am—and that's saying something.

But writing for money is way better than many jobs I've had. I much prefer it to practicing law, bussing dishes, serving drinks, stocking groceries, and making pizzas. When I'm having a rough day, I think back to my legal career and remember the dread I experienced every morning except Saturday and Sunday. Knowing that I hated my job, hated what my job entailed, and hated how I spent the working hours keeps me in the freelance game.

I'm not saying you have to be thrilled to decide to write for money, or that you must approach every day as a wonderful adventure. Maybe you're in desperate circumstances and you really need writing for money to work for you. Maybe you're a depressive by nature. But just remember that what you believe about yourself tends to happen.

I know a writer who's been freelancing much longer than I am. She's actually quite talented (I've read some of her work) but she is the walking definition of the "Debby Downer" character from *Saturday Night Live*. I've met her only once, briefly, but I feel that I know her. I've read her posts on online forums for years and they always involve whining, bitching, or complaining. She's had some success as a freelancer but I doubt that any more is headed her way. Every post she writes is bitter and some are truly venomous. I wouldn't want to be her friend, and I wouldn't want to work with her either. And **that** is my point.

Yes, editors want writers who can deliver the work. But your words are only part of what you offer a client. Your responsiveness, your creativity, your professionalism, and yes, your attitude all make a difference.

Maybe like me, you have natural PMA. But even us "glass-half-fulls" have bad days, too. And when I do, I don't want to write for money anymore. (But then what the hell am I going to do?) So I use a coping mechanism. I play the "worst case scenario" game.

Let's say an editor is unhappy with my work. Sorry to say, that has happened to me. Multiple times. My gut reaction is always a bit melodramatic (that's where my son gets it from!) and goes along these lines:

I suck. My work sucks. I'm a fraud and the only reason I've made it this far is through circumstances of luck both blind and dumb. My client thinks I'm an idiot. I am an idiot. He'll never work with me again. He's going to tell everyone what an idiot I am. He'll even Tweet it! I'll never get another assignment again. My freelance career is over. I suck. I suck so bad. I am a freaking idiot…

Are you surprised? Well, that's what an optimist like me feels like when I screw up. But I can imagine that in a similar situation, someone with a more negative outlook would think: *I suck. My work sucks. I'm a fraud and the only reason I've made it this far is through circumstances of luck both blind and dumb.*

My client thinks I'm an idiot. I am an idiot. He'll never work with me again. He'll tell everyone what an idiot I am. He'll even Tweet it! I'll never get another assignment again. My freelance career is over. I suck. I suck so bad. I am a freaking idiot...

In other words, no matter how positive you are—or how negative—there will be times when you doubt yourself, or your abilities, or your stamina. All normal. Let yourself thrash around in your misery for a little bit (I'll give you 20 minutes) and then take a deep breath and figure out what you can do to address the situation. Maybe you need to rewrite the article. Maybe you need to find some new sources. Maybe you need to cut bait with a an editor you've worked for in the past but who constantly criticizes your work. There's always *something* you can do, even if it means just accepting something crappy happened and you're going to put it out of your mind. That's much better than continuing to twist yourself into knots over it.

Develop Resilience

Good things happen when you write for money. You sell an article. You get paid. You see your byline. You feel smart and accomplished. You sell another article. You get paid again. You feel even smarter and more accomplished. And so on. Those are good things. But writing for money means that some bad things are going to happen too. You can't control that. All you can control is how you react and respond to those events—and develop what psychologists call resilience in the process. Resilience is, in my words, **your ability to bounce back when shit happens**. (Pardon my French, as my grandmother used to say.)

And while resilience appears to have a genetic component (some of us just have more of it), it turns out, resilience can be learned. I know. That's how I got mine.

The first year of fulltime freelancing, I sent out more than 200 queries to potential markets. (This is including resubs, but that's still a lot of pitching.) You know how many of them actually sold? Are you ready? Thirteen.

Thirteen out of more than 200. That's not an impressive number. If I started out freelancing today and had that kind of result, I don't know that I could, or would, stick with it.

But receiving so many "bongs" (that's what I call rejections) thickened my skin. I stopped taking rejection personally. Yes, I was still annoyed. Disappointed. Discouraged. Frequently disgusted and occasionally depressed. But I knew it wasn't a rejection of me, only of my idea. (And looking back, many of my queries were terrible. They lacked focus, they were poorly researched, they weren't written with the magazine's audience in mind. No wonder they failed!)

By using the 24-hour rule, I turned each of those bongs into two opportunities. I kept pitching. I kept trying. Yes, I was discouraged but I kept my hand in, so to speak. And eventually I started getting assignments—not only because I kept pitching but **because my queries got better**. Much better. By my second year of freelancing, about one-quarter of my pitches sold, and that percentage continued to climb. (Today, more than half of the articles I pitch sell—and that's a percentage I'm very happy with.)

I tell new writers that they will spend most of their time marketing until they start getting assignments. And that marketing doesn't pay off until you get work. Well, that's not quite true. Because the marketing you do makes you a better marketer. Write a lot of queries with the goal of improving your queries, and you will write better queries! And **better queries=more assignments**.

The same goes for the actual work you're producing for clients. During my early years of freelancing, I wrote some articles that were not very good. I'm being honest here. But those articles worked fine for the markets they were written for, and my editors were happy with them. (And some of those markets were national magazines!) More importantly, actually writing those articles helped make me a better writer, which led to more work, more assignments, more confidence, you name it.

But let's say you're starting out. You don't have that confidence yet. Maybe you don't have any. I'm going to help you create some. Let's say you're pitching an online market that's new to you, with a query letter. You wrote a killer query. It was a great fit for the market. Yet you got bonged.

Even when you're doing good work, you're going to get rejected. That is part of freelancing. I told you earlier to expect it. But you also have to learn to shake it off and move on. The best way for me to shake it off is to resub the idea somewhere else. The freelance ocean is full of fish, or rather, markets. Choose another possibility to pitch.

I also remind myself that it may only have been my idea that didn't work for the editor. So I'll use my 24-hour rule (choose whatever time period works for *you*) and send another pitch to the same editor. I feel better, and you will too, simply because you haven't let the editor have the last word ("no"). And if she bongs that idea, too? Well, I repeat as necessary—unless I decide this market isn't worth my while. Then I imagine saying, "See ya!" and move on to more promising pastures. I'm not letting the editor dictate my life. I'm *choosing* not to pitch the market anymore, which makes me feel more in control, and at least a little bit better.

And if I need to, I vent. Sometimes I need to get a little bit Debby Downer myself. I need to, well, bitch to somebody. If my husband's around, great. (Maybe not for him, but we're talking about **me** here, remember?) If not, I'll call a close friend—maybe a freelancer, maybe not—and ask permission to complain. I'll say, "Hey, are you busy? Can I host a bitch session for five minutes?" and then I launch right into it. Then it's my friend's turn! Bitch sessions aren't for everyone—I only share those negative feelings with those closest to me (I know, you're thinking, "lucky them!") but they save my sanity and help me readjust my perspective.

I wish I could say bad things never happen to me as a writer. Alas, they do. But I've learned how to handle them. I've become resilient, and that isn't through the good things happening. It's because of the shitty things.

So when a shitty thing happens, remind yourself it's good. It's making you more resilient as a writer, and that's always a positive thing.

Get out of your Chair

If you decide you want to continue to write for money, it's not enough to work efficiently, create relationships with clients, and treat your writing like a business. You have to take care of your body as well.

I'm fortunate in that other than a series of running-related injuries, I've been fairly healthy since I became self-employed. Yes, I get colds occasionally (that's a given when you have small humans in your home), but overall I'm sturdy and energetic.

There's a reason for that (besides my Irish and German peasant genes). I exercise.

Couch potatoes, don't roll your eyes or skip ahead. Yes, I'm also an ACE-certified personal trainer. But I'm not going to show up at your home and drag you away from your desk. What I will say is that if you want to improve your writing, your stamina, even your attitude, get your butt out of your chair occasionally. Make time to do something physical at least once a day.

I look at exercise as a way burning off the mental fog that collects every morning like mist on a lake. Without sweating, that fog doesn't dissipate—it grows. For me, it manifests in anxious thoughts, a racing mind, and an inability to concentrate. Working out first thing in the morning costs me some of my work time, but it more than makes up for it with my increased productivity when I am working.

Everybody—and everybody's body—is different. I have only two requirements for whatever physical activity you choose:

1. You must enjoy it (at least most of the time)
2. You must expend more energy doing it than you do at your desk.

It's that simple. I've met hundreds of freelancers over the years and many are dedicated athletes of some kind. Some run. Some do yoga. Some swim. Some bike. Some lift weights. Some take kick-boxing or Spinning or Zumba classes. Some simply walk regularly.

But they do *something* that challenges their physical bodies, and that makes a difference. Research has proven that regular exercise:

- Reduces anxiety;
- Alleviates depression;
- Improves mood;
- Improves cognitive ability;
- Improves the ability to focus on a specific task; and
- Enhances memory.

Wow! So you can be a less anxious, less depressed, more positive, more creative, more focused, *and* more productive writer, all by exercising! That's enough for me, but that's only the beginning. Then there's those physical benefits too. Exercise burns calories, strengthens your muscles, improves your posture, reduces your risk of heart disease (the number one killer of writers—and everyone else) and just about every other condition you can think of.

Look at the time you spend working out as an aspect of successfully writing for money, just as you would researching markets or brainstorming ideas. It's that essential.

Okay, I'm done lecturing you about working out. (Really.) I just want you to start thinking about your body as an essential part of your business—it's not something that can be overlooked or ignored. I know that if I go without physical activity—whether it's running or biking or going to yoga—for more than a day or two, I'm less able to focus on my work. And because I'm all about working productively, I need to be able to focus and churn out words when I sit down for my allotted work time.

Your time to write for money is limited. Taking care of your physical body will help you make more of that time. That's another promise I feel confident making you. Now, I'm off to practice what I preach and take my dog for a walk before I return to work on this book.

Get Some Friends

There's another factor that will impact your success when you write for money. It's social support, a/k/a your friends, family, and fellow writers. When you decide to write for money, you're stretching yourself. You're doing something that you haven't done before. You're setting yourself up for rejection, failure, depression, you name it. So it helps to have someone—hopefully more than one someone—in your corner, so to speak.

When I started freelancing, I was living with the man who's now my husband. I worked fulltime as a lawyer and used some of my "free time" to research markets and write queries, articles, and essays. The time I spent on my writing meant I had less time to spend with him, but he was okay with that. And when I decided to ditch the law to write fulltime, he was okay with that, too. He was actually more than okay. He supported my decision 100 percent, even though I told him I'd be quite broke for a while (and I was).

I can't imagine making that transition if he hadn't been supportive, much less if he had been critical or hostile about my major career change. It didn't matter that he wasn't a writer. He understood that getting my work published was incredibly important to me, and he supported that—even when it took me several years to really get my business going.

But I need more than Erik. I need friends who are writers themselves. Friends who "get it." I started out with no writer support system but over time, I created one by attending conferences, joining "listservs" (the predecessors to online bulletin boards), and teaching classes. I joined organizations like the American Society of Journalists and Authors, and an online community called Freelance Success, where I connected with dozens of like-minded writers. (In fact, Freelance Success, which I mentioned in chapter 2, is one of the most valuable resources I can recommend to freelancers who are serious about writing nonfiction articles for print and online markets. It's $99/year, but the market guide, supportive community, and online bulletin boards make it well worth the cost. And as you'll see in chapter 6, it's a business expense you can write off!)

While I want you to focus on getting your first few assignments at first, I also encourage you to start creating your own community of writers. There are dozens of blogs for writers who write for money; some of my favorites include:

- All Freelance Writing, http://allfreelancewriting.com/blog;
- Dollars and Deadlines, http://dollarsanddeadlines.blogspot.com (Yup, that's mine!);
- Guerilla Freelancing, www.guerillafreelancing.com;
- Make a Living Writing, www.makealivingwriting.com/;
- The Renegade Writer, www.therenegadewriter.com;
- The Urban Muse, www.urbanmusewriter.com; and
- WordCount--Freelancing in the Digital Age, http://michellerafter.com/.

Pick several to follow and comment on posts occasionally. You'll not only learn more about freelancing in general, you'll also start to recognize names and get to know some of your fellow writers. You can also use social media to start creating relationships with other writers. [See chapter 12 for more on your online presence.]

Don't be afraid to reach out to other writers, even if they're more experienced than you are. We were all clueless beginners at one point. But don't expect a stranger to spoon-feed you secrets of her success or to hand over her editors' names or recommend you to her agent.

If you're going to contact another writer, I suggest you keep your email brief; let her know why you're contacting her; and express your appreciation for her time. It's okay, in my opinion, to ask for a favor as long as it's a small one. Just keep in mind that the person you're contacting is under no obligation to do anything for you, even reply to your email.

On the other hand, some of my long-standing relationships with my writing peers started with an email. Here's an example of the way you might reach out to a fellow writer you'd like to connect with:

Subject line: We write for the same magazine

Dear Leslie:

I've seen your name in *For the Bride*, a magazine I've written for before. I just wanted to email and introduce myself; I'm a fulltime freelancer who writes about bridal, health, fitness, and nutrition topics. I'm also teaching a class for new writers next month. Would you mind if I asked you a couple of questions about how you approach your freelance business that I could share with my students? I'd be happy to call at your convenience or send you them by email if that works better for you.

If you're interested, please let me know. If not, no problem, and I'll continue to watch for your name in *For the Bride*!

Thanks so much and have a great day!

All my best,
Kelly James-Enger

Note that I haven't asked for the sun, moon, and stars. I've made a reasonable request, and opened the door to a relationship. Maybe she'll get back to me; maybe she won't. If she does, great; otherwise I won't take it personally.

I said earlier that you need basic writing skills to write for money. You need to know how to pitch, research, and craft articles. If you also strive to have the four elements discussed in this chapter—a positive attitude, resilience, physical activity, and a freelancing friend or two—you'll boost your chances of success.

CHAPTER 5
Get a Contract Clue: What Every Writer Should Know

Chances are if you're a writer, you also consider yourself somewhat creative. If you're going to write for money, however, that creativity will take you only so far. You also need at least a minimal understanding of what that contract you're signing actually means.

Many writers don't even bother to read their contracts--and even if they do, they don't understand what they're reading. Consider this chapter the least you need to know about contracts, from the perspective of a longtime freelancer (and former lawyer). Just don't consider it legal advice—I left that field a long time ago!

Contract Basics

First off, when you enter into a contract with an editor, the contract specifies which rights you are selling to your work. According to the copyright law, every time you create a written work (get it down "in fixed form," whether that's on a legal pad or an iPad), you've also created copyright to the work at the same time. I could write several chapters on copyright law, but let's keep it simple. As a new freelancer, all you need to know is that copyright law refers to a "bundle of rights" that attach to any piece of writing that is in fixed form.

Those rights include but are not limited to:

- The right to publish the work for the first time in a North American serial (or publication), often called "first N.A. serial rights";
- The right to publish the work online;
- The right to reprint the work;
- The right to publish the work in a database, directory, or in a book;
- The right to create a movie based on the work;
- The right to create an app based on the work;
- The right to put the work on a poster, a tee-shirt, or a towel;
- And any other right you can imagine.

The idea I want you to grasp is that this "bundle" includes every right imaginable, but unless a publisher or client buys "all rights," a written contract will enumerate the rights that are being sold or transferred.

The rest remain your property [of the rights not enumerated]. It's not that complicated.

If you don't have a written contract, it's presumed that you're selling one-time rights to an article. But I suggest that if you fail to receive a contract from your editor, you provide your own. Then you have written evidence of what you agreed to; this is especially important if you have to chase payment down.

Your contract should include the name of the parties (namely you, and the publication you're writing for); the date; the description of the work you're doing (i.e., your assignment); the deadline; the money you're being paid; and the rights being purchased. It needn't include anything else.

Here's a simple contract you're free to adopt as your own:

THIS AGREEMENT is made on the _____ day of _____, 2012, by and among EDITOR of PUBLICATION OF CITY, STATE (hereinafter referred to as EDITOR) and Kelly James-Enger of Downers Grove, Illinois (hereinafter referred to as James-Enger). The parties agree as follows:

1. Subject to the terms and conditions herein, EDITOR and James-Enger agree that James-Enger will write an article of ___ words on the subject of _____ for EDITOR. The deadline for the article to be submitted shall be_____, 2012.
2. The fee for the article will be $_____, payable to James-Enger upon acceptance of the article.
3. EDITOR is purchasing the following rights to the article: _____.
4. This agreement shall be construed in accordance with the laws of the State of Illinois.

IN WITNESS WHEREOF, the parties hereto have set their hands on the date first above specified.

_____

EDITOR/PUBLICATION
[contact information]

_____

Kelly James-Enger
[contact information]

You'll also find a letter of agreement, which operates as a contract, in chapter 9. 10

Contract Provisions

See how simple a contract can be? And in some instances, your editor will have a short, relatively simple contract. In others, though, you'll face pages of provisions using terms you've never heard of and struggle to understand.

While every contract is different, there are seven major topics you may see addressed that you should understand, so let's take a look at some specific types of contract provisions and what they mean.

Rights Provisions

One of the most important sections of the contract is the one that specifies which rights you're selling. As a writer, the fewer rights you sell, the better, but keep in mind that some work has more resale potential than others. [We'll talk more about reselling work in chapter 12.] So, for example, an article I wrote on how exercise can help you lose weight has more "legs" than the piece I did for a trade magazine aimed at retail grocers about how to sell more meat at their butcher counters.

And the fact is that more markets want all rights. Yes, you can try to negotiate to retain some rights, but be aware that publishers are definitely moving in that direction. (Don't worry—we'll talk about how to negotiate more writer-friendly contracts later in this chapter.)

Here's a typical rights provision you might see, with my comments in brackets:

You grant ABC Publications First North American Serial Rights as well as nonexclusive electronic rights to use this article on any Web sites owned by ABC publications. [First North American serial rights means the right to publish the piece for the first time in a magazine in the US, Canada, or Mexico. This is pretty standard with print magazines. The company is also purchasing electronic rights to any of its websites. Because it hasn't specified a particular time period, it's asking for electronic rights forever. "Nonexclusive" means that you as the writer retain electronic rights to the piece as well.]

Here's another rights provision:

Author conveys to MM the exclusive license to publish the article, worldwide, in print media (including, but not limited to, ABC Magazine), in any electronic media authorized by MM, and in reprints published by MM. [In other words, this is asking for all rights as it's an "exclusive" license.] The rights herein granted include the right to use Author's name, approved biography, credit line, likeness, and any portion of the article in connection with the publication, advertising, and promotion of the article; and to make such other promotional use of the article as MM deems necessary. [The magazine is purchasing the right to use your name and a photo of you—even a bad one!— to promote the piece. This may not be a big deal, but if you're writing a piece under a pseudonym or don't want your byline or likeness connected with the piece or the market, you'd want to strike this language.]

And one more:

Author sells to publisher (a) first periodical rights; (b) the right to reprint, adapt, condense, or translate the Work in any editions of MAGAZINE; (c) the right to publish the Work in publications of PUBLISHING COMPANY; (d) the right to publish or license the Work in whole or in part, in electronic, digital, or computerized form; (e) syndication and reprint rights, for which Author will receive 50% of net proceeds. [So, the publisher is buying the right not only to publish the story in this magazine, but in any other of its magazines as well. It is also buying electronic rights and the right to syndicate the article. Note though that it doesn't ask for "exclusive" syndication and reprint rights, so you as the Author would still be able to resell this article once it was first published.]

So far these provisions have been pretty straightforward. Let's look at one that's more complex (I've found that the larger the corporation that owns the publication, the longer and more convoluted the contract becomes). Take a deep breath—this is a long one:

In consideration for the payments to you described in Section 3 above and in this Section, you hereby grant TPG the following rights with respect to the Article:
  a. the right to publish the article in ABC magazine, including all print and digital versions [so the publisher can run the piece in print and online];
  b. the right, for an amount equal to 50% of any fee received by TPG, to authorize the republication of the Article, in part or in its entirety, in any English and foreign language newspapers and periodicals; [this means the publisher can offer reprint rights to the piece, and you'll receive half of what the publisher receives];
  c. The right, for an amount equal to 15% of the fee set for in the first sentence of Section 3 above, to republish the Article, in part or in its entirety, in DEF magazine, including all print and digital versions (in which event TPG will have all of the same rights with respect to the Article for DEF magazine as those granted hereunder for ABC magazine in parts 4 and 5 [the publisher wants the right to run the story in another one of its publications, for a mere 15% more than what it paid for the original piece];
  d. The right to republish the Article as part of the issue of ABC magazine in which it first appeared (including, without limitation, any revision of such issue) [in my opinion, this clause is unnecessary because of section "a," but publishers like to make sure they have every possibility covered];
  e. The right to republish the Article, in part or in its entirety, in advertising

and promotional materials for TPG [pretty standard clause];

f. The right to republish and authorize republication of the Article, in part or in its entirety, in any English and foreign language reprints and collections of material (including, without limitation, custom-published projects, and anthologies), including all print and digital versions thereof and Additional Electronic works (defined below), that bear any "TPG" brands [again, the publisher wants to be able to reprint the story whenever and wherever it wants];

g. The rights, for a one-time payment equal to $15 for a department Article or $25 for a feature Article, to republish and authorize republication of the Article, in part or in its entirety, in digitized form in any and all Additional Electronic Works. "Additional Electronic Works" is defined as electronic works other than digital versions of a magazine or Collection, including, without limitation, all ABC or DEF-branded online sites or areas or any other English and foreign language materials transmitted, distributed, displayed, performed or otherwise communicated (collectively, "Published") through any and all magnetic, digital, laser, optical, wire line, wireless, cable modem and satellite based means, and through all current and future protocols and networks. [The poor lawyer writing this in the mid 2000s was trying to figure out every type of technology that could be developed. Regardless, for a whopping $15 or $25, the publisher owns the right to publish the piece through any electronic means. Get it?]

h. All rights to the Article include the right to translate the Article. All rights are hereby granted by you exclusively to TPG, in all media now known or hereafter devised throughout the world, from the date of the creation of the Article until the expiration of the 60-day period immediately following the "publication date" of the Article in ABC magazine. [This is an exclusivity provision, which we'll discuss more in a bit.] For purposes of the foregoing, the "publication date" is the first day of the month printed on the cover of the issue of Parenting magazine in which the Article first appears (or, for bi-monthly issues, the first day of the second month printed on the cover). Following the expiration of the above-described 60-day period, all of TPG's rights to the Article, as described above, are hereby granted by you to TPG non-exclusively, in all media known or hereafter devised, throughout the world and in perpetuity unless otherwise specified in this Agreement. All rights in the Article not expressly granted to TPG by you hereunder shall be retained by you, provided, however, that you agree that TPG will receive suitable credit upon the exercise by you of any such retained rights. [Oh, good! So any rights not described already are retained by you—as long as you make sure that the publisher is credited whenever you resell or reuse the work.]

Now you should have an understanding of what these rights provisions mean, so let's move on to something just as important—getting paid.

Payment Provisions

The contract should specify exactly what you're being paid for the article you're writing. It's almost always a per-word rate (e.g. $1/word) although for blog posts and some other online publications, you may be paid a flat rate (say, $250 for a blog post of 500 to 700 words.). Make sure when you receive your contract that the amount is what you agreed to via phone or email. If it's not, cross out the incorrect amount and write the correct amount above it, along with your initials and the date.

But it's not only what you're going to be paid but *when*. As a freelancer, there are two basic ways to be paid—"on acceptance" or "on publication." "On acceptance" means that you're paid after your editor agrees that your piece has met her specifications. (That doesn't mean you get paid right away, though usually you can expect payment in 30 to 45 days.) "On publication" means you don't get paid until the piece runs, and this is a problem for several reasons.

First, there's no guarantee that the publication will run your story. What if your editor changes her mind, or decides the piece is no longer timely? Then the story doesn't get published, which means you don't get paid. Second, what if the story gets pushed back for months? Then you're waiting to get paid for work you did through no fault of your own. That's why whenever you can, you want your contract to specify that you'll be paid on acceptance.

Here's an example of a payment provision:

MM shall pay author $1,200, for an article of 1,200 words accepted for publication by MM within 30 days of acceptance. If the article is not accepted, Author will be paid a kill fee of 20%. MM shall have no other rights to the article. [The last two lines refer to a kill fee, which we'll discuss below.]

I've found that it's rare to see a contract that specifies when you'll be paid (e.g., "within 30 days of acceptance.") But do look for the words "on acceptance" or "paid on acceptance." If a contract specifies "on publication," don't be afraid to ask whether you can change that language to "on acceptance" as it is more common among publications.

In addition to the payment provision, you may see a provision about expenses. In the golden days of freelancing, writers got to go places. Lots of places. And publishers paid for it. Today, not so much. But you may see a clause like this:

Publisher shall reimburse Author for reasonable and necessary expenses incurred in preparation of the Work, provided that Publisher approves such expenses in advance, and Author provides Publisher with itemized receipts therefor.

Fair enough. So what might those expenses include? In the past, I expensed photocopies, long-distance charges, and travel costs if related to the article. Today's technology has changed that--I don't need to call Asia long-distance; I can Skype for free. And most of the work I do requires little in "expenses." But if you're going to incur expenses related to the story, then yes, you want your publisher to reimburse you for them. Fair enough, right?

Kill Fee Provisions

A "kill fee" is an amount of money a publisher pays you if the powers that be (namely, your editor--or possibly your editor's editor) decides he no longer wants to publish this story. Maybe it's no longer timely. Maybe the piece didn't meet your editor's specifications. Maybe he changed her mind. Hell, maybe you just wrote a crappy story. That doesn't matter with a kill fee. The editor "kills" the story and pays the kill fee.

Here's the thing. Some writers hate kill fees because it gives an editor carte blanche to kill a story that may have been perfectly serviceable. And if that's the case, the writer should be paid for the piece. Don't you agree? It doesn't matter--not all contracts contain a kill fee provision, but some do and some editors do use them unjustly. Life's not always fair for us freelancers.

Here's an example of a kill fee provision:

Publisher has the right not to publish the Work at its discretion. [In other words, the Publisher doesn't need a reason--even a flimsy one--to kill a piece.] If Publisher does not accept the Work, it shall pay Author a kill fee of twenty-five percent (25%) of the Original Fee in lieu of the Original Fee, in which case all rights in and to the Work shall revert immediately to Author.

Read the last part of the last sentence closely. It includes the upside of the kill fee provision. The rights to the piece are yours again, so you're free to turn around and pitch and hopefully sell the article somewhere else. On the other hand, you may not be able to sell the piece--and then you're left with nothing more than 25 percent of your original fee and a bad taste in your mouth.

Here's another kill fee provision:

On receiving the Work in a condition acceptable to Publisher, Publisher will pay Author $600 for rights as outlined in Paragraph 5. Publisher will pay author a kill fee of 33% of the fee(s), and rights to the Work revert to Author, if Author fails in Publisher's judgment to deliver of Work of quality similar to what which routinely appears in MAGAZINE.

Once again, the kill fee provision can be enacted by the Publisher if the work isn't up to snuff, at least in your editor's opinion.

I don't have a problem with kill fee provisions, though I agree that they can be abused. Do a good job, give the editor what he wants, and hopefully you'll never have to worry about one. And in the event that you do have a story killed, take the kill fee and pitch the story somewhere else. (Don't tell the editor that your piece was rejected by another publication! Simply start fresh with a pitch to a similar market.)

Cooperation Provisions

Yes, you're writing the piece, and your name, or byline will most likely appear with it. But that doesn't mean that you have any say in what the final version of the story looks like. In many contracts, you'll find a clause that asks you to edit or rework the piece at the editor's request; you may also find a clause where the publisher specifically retains the right to determine how the final piece will read.

Take a look:

...Author shall cooperate in the Magazine's normal editing process and shall make such changes to the Work as may be reasonably requested prior to publication.

Final editing and illustrations to the Work shall be the sole discretion of the Magazine.

In other words, if your editor does a bang-up job to your story and it reads better than you could have imagined, great news. If your editor mangles your story and that's what is approved to run, that's what will be published. You have zero control over it.

Really, really unhappy with what an editor did? Mortified by the idea that your name will appear next to the mangled story? You can take the fairly dramatic step of requesting that your byline be removed. That lets your editor know you're extremely unhappy with how the story turned out--so much so that you don't want anyone to know you wrote it!

I know a handful of writers who have employed this technique, but it doesn't endear you to your editor). My opinion? If you work with an editor who trashes your work, don't use it as a clip (it's not a sample of your best work, after all), and move on. My attitude? Why burn a bridge if you don't need to?

"Restrictive Covenant" Provisions

You've already seen a contract that has an exclusivity provision, but let's take a closer look at them. Publications get sensitive about writers covering the same material, especially for their competitors. So you may see language like:

Author shall not write, publish or cooperate in the publication of another work in any medium on the same or a similar subject as the Work from the date hereof until ninety (90) days after the on-sale date of the issue of the Magazine in which the Work is first published, unless Publisher provides Author with written consent thereto.

Get the idea? The magazine doesn't want to get "scooped," or to see you writing about the same thing, at least not for three months after it runs the story. I can understand that, but what's "a similar subject?" If you write about technology, for example, and you do a piece on great cooking apps for a magazine, does that mean you can't write about apps at all for 90 days?

That seems unfair, especially if you, like many freelancers, specialize. Another issue is the time frame--the publication could fail to run the story for months and in the meantime, you're hamstrung from covering the subject (or similar subject). Yes, this provision gives you an out--if you get written consent, no problem. But what if you don't? I try to strike these provisions whenever I can. If I can't get rid of them, I keep close tabs on when stories are running so I don't wind up violating my own contract.

Warranty Provisions

You wrote this article, right? You know you did. But the contract may include language where you state that that's the case.

A writer's warranty provision may look like this:

Author warrants that: the Work is or will be Author's original work; Author has the right to grant the rights granted herein; there has been no prior sale, publication or transfer of rights to the Work or any part of it; the Work contains no libelous material, to the best of Author's knowledge; and publication of the Work will not infringe upon any third party's copyright or other rights, including, without limitation, the rights of privacy and publicity. Author will fully cooperate with the Magazine in responding to and defending against any third party claim relating to the Work.

This is a big paragraph but in short it means that you're guaranteeing that you in fact wrote the assignment and that it's original (not work that's appeared somewhere else) and that you didn't do anything illegal or unethical in the process. And I trust you won't, right?

Here's another example:

You represent and warrant that the Article shall be wholly original material not published elsewhere (except for material in the public domain or used with permission of its owner), will not infringe any copyright, and will not constitute a defamation, or invasion of the right of privacy or publicity, or infringement of any other right of any other kind, of any third party. [Standard stuff, seeking confirmation that you wrote the piece yourself and that you didn't libel or plagiarize anyone. In this contract, there's no indemnification provision, but it would commonly follow or be incorporated into a section with this language.]

Indemnification Provisions

Now that you've seen some typical warranty provisions, let's talk about indemnification provisions and what they mean. Let's say that you turn in a story that isn't your original work, or that you defame or plagiarize someone—and that leads to a legal claim against the publisher.

An indemnification takes your warranty a step further. Not only do you guarantee that your work is original and won't subject the publisher to any legal claims, you indemnify, or protect, the publisher from claims or damages that may result. In other words, if you screw up, you promise you'll make things right for the publisher.

Here's what an indemnification provision may look like. Note that the warranty provision precedes it:

> I warrant that the work is original, that I am the sole author, that I have not assigned nor licensed any right in it to any other party which would violate this agreement and that reproduction and distribution of the Work does not infringe on any other party's existing copyright. Additionally, I will indemnify and hold harmless ABC against any resulting cost, loss, damage, expense and judgment (if any) resulting from **aforementioned breach** [my emphasis], including without limitation settlement payments and reasonable attorneys' fees, charges and disbursements.

This indemnification doesn't bother me as much as some others because here you only indemnify the publisher for breaching the agreement—in other words, infringing on someone else's copyright. Well, if I did that, I'm willing to indemnify the publisher—because I know I'm not going to do that. And I know you're going to be a smart, ethical freelancer and not do it either.

Contrast that language with the following:

> You represent and warrant that the article will be original work by you and accurate, will not have been previously published in any form, and will not infringe upon the personal or proprietary rights or give rise to any third party claim, including but not limited to claims based on copyright, defamation, physical injury, or invasion of privacy and publicity. [This is the warranty language.] In addition, in the event that any complaint or claim relating to the article is made by any third party at any time, whether a formal legal complaint or otherwise, you will fully cooperate with Publisher in responding to and defending against such a claim. [Fair enough.]

In the above paragraph, you're warranting that your work won't open the publisher up to any claims, but if there is a claim, you'll cooperate with the defense of it. This is completely reasonable, in my opinion.

Now let's look at a longer provision:

Author represents and warrants that any article Author may present under this Agreement shall be Author's wholly original work, not previously published in any media, in whole or in part; that the work will infringe any person's or entity's copyright, trademarks, service mark, or other proprietary rights, and will not constitute defamation, invasion of the rights of privacy, or infringement of any other rights of any kind of any third party. In the event that any threat, demand, claim, or action is asserted against MM or any of its affiliates, or their officers, directors, or employees, by any person or entity alleging copyright, trademark, or service mark infringement; unfair competition; misuse of proprietary ideas of expression; defamation; invasion of privacy; or any other claim arising out of MM's publication of Author's article, Author shall defend, indemnify and hold harmless MM, its affiliates, and their officers, directors, and employees from any and all liabilities, expenses, costs, damages, settlements, or judgments, including attorney fees, incurred in connection with such threat, demand, claim or action **if Author is shown to have violated his agreements as judged in a court of law** [my emphasis].

Scared by the breadth of this language? I would be too, except for the last clause, "if Author is shown to have violated his agreements as judged in a court of law." In other words, the Publisher has to not only be sued because of your work—it has to be proven that you violated your contract for you to indemnify the publisher. That certainly seems reasonable to me because I know I'm not going to violate my contract, and I trust that you won't either.

However, there are broad indemnification provisions that I try to strike or change. Look at this clause:

Author shall defend, indemnify and hold harmless ABC company, its affiliates, and their officers, directors, and employees from **any and all claims** [my emphasis], liabilities, expenses, costs, damages, settlements, or judgments, including attorney fees, incurred in connection with such threat, demand, claim or action, that arise out of ABC's publication of Author's article.

The phrase that worries me is "any and all claims." This is the United States. Anyone can sue anyone for anything. It's not that expensive or difficult to bring a lawsuit, and many suits are settled for "nuisance value." It's cheaper to settle even a bogus suit than to pay the cost of defending it. Yet under the broad language of this provision, you'd be on the hook. Is that right? No. Is it fair? No. And remember you're a writer, not an insurer. Strike these clauses if you can.

In addition to these seven major topics, you'll often see provisions that specify what state's law may govern the contract; that parties have to agree to arbitration in the event of a disagreement; and that the agreement is binding on successors to the contract. None of those clauses should give you much pause.

Changing Contract Terms

Okay. Now you have a better understanding of what contract issues you should be aware of. So what happens when you're given a contract with language you want to change?

First, decide what is most important to you. If you want to retain rights to your work to be able to resell it in the future, you won't want to agree to an "all rights" contract. If an agreement has a heinous indemnification provision and you know you're going to lie awake worrying about someone suing the publication over your story, you'll want to strike that language. Or maybe you specialize in a subject area and you don't want to be prevented from writing about the same subject while you wait for a story to run. You have to know what you want—and what you're willing to accept—before you attempt to negotiate a better deal.

Next, take a deep breath. I know asking to change a contract is scary when you're a new writer! As you'll see in the next chapter, I didn't even ask for more money from a market until I'd been freelancing fulltime for more than a year! I took anything that was offered and said, "Thank you!" (That's not a great business strategy, by the way.)

You have two basic ways to negotiate a contract change—call your editor and explain what changes you'd like, and why. Or email her and do the same thing. I know, most of you are thinking, "Email! I'll email!" Let me suggest, though, that a phone call is often a smarter choice. When you're talking to someone by phone, the person can hear your vocal inflections and tone of voice. Via email, your words are only that—your words. It's easy to misinterpret your meaning on the other end.

Next chapter, I'll talk more about the TEA method, which I use to ask for more money. TEA stands for **Thank, Explain, Ask**. I also use this method to change contract language. For example, "John, I'm looking forward to writing this piece and appreciate you thinking of me for the story. [Thank.] That being said, I noticed your contract asks for all rights. I like to retain rights to my work so I can resell stories in the future. Reprints are kind of my freelance pension plan. [Explain.] Would it be all right if you purchased first North American Serial rights and electronic rights instead, and I could retain the rights? Or could I retain nonexclusive reprint rights? [Ask.]"

See how TEA works? Now the editor may say yes to my suggested change. If he does, I'll change the contract, initial and date it and send it back to him. I got what I wanted! Victory!

If he says no, well, I have to decide if I'm still willing to do the story. If you are someone who is new to writing for money, I suggest you be willing. I signed all-rights contracts with horrible, unfair (and probably unenforceable) indemnification provisions early on in my career. I didn't care about contracts! (Let's forget the fact I'd been, you know, a contract attorney before.) I cared about getting assignments, making money, forging relationships. And I think that was the right approach.

I know I'm going to get at least one email from a writer who says I should be ashamed of myself for suggesting that freelancers take whatever crappy contracts they're offered. That I should tell you to take a stand and refuse to write for a market unless its contract is fair. And I will admit that yes, I've turned down assignments because I couldn't get an editor to concede to my suggested changes.

But I live in this place called reality. And the reality is that contracts are getting grabbier. Publications want more rights. They don't care about what you, the writer, wants. So you may have to suck it up and sign it, especially as a new writer. That's just how it is.

I've included a chapter on contracts because I want you to be a well-informed freelancer. I do! And I want you to know that you can ask for contracts to be changed. But the editor may refuse to change them. Then you have to decide whether you're willing to take that particular deal, **for now** at least, while you build your freelance career. As time goes on, you may not have to sign crappy contracts. But as a new writer, you probably will have to. Does that make you a sell-out? I don't think so. I think it makes you practical.

Bottom line: understand that contracts are typically written for the benefit of the markets you're writing for, and know what you're signing. Don't be afraid to try to change a contract, but if you can't, consider the value of the assignment—and where you are in your writing career—before you walk away. That kind of "realistic thinking" (as opposed to the magical kind) will help you go from unpublished to published, and from newbie to successful self-employed writer.

CHAPTER 6:
Straight Talk about Money—and Taxes

Now that you've learned about contracts—and what to look for—let's talk about something that many writers shy away from. It's the subject of money.

I've met a lot of writers who simply aren't comfortable talking about money—or even thinking about money, at least as it applies to their writing. Get over that idea. There are writers who make a six-figure living. There are those who make a few thousand dollars a year.

Are the writers who make more money better writers? Are they better people? Maybe. Maybe not. But they may have more experience than writers who are starting out, or they may have expertise in a certain subject area (say, writing white papers or ghostwriting business books) that commands higher fees, or they may work more efficiently, or they may have diversified their businesses so they have money coming in from a variety of different clients. In later chapters we'll talk about all of these strategies.

For now, all you need to remember is that you **want to make money** from your writing—and **there's nothing wrong with that**. Being paid doesn't devalue your work or make you less of an artist than someone who remains "pure" and unconcerned about money. Hey, you don't have to talk about money with other writers if you don't want to. You can keep that to yourself—maybe you're more comfortable with that, and that's fine.

You bought this book because you want to make money selling your work. So you may be wondering how much you can make. In the last sixteen years, I've made as little as $17,100 working as a fulltime freelancer and I've broken the six-figure mark. (For the record, I prefer the former.) I've averaged about $50,000/year, and that's including the years I've worked part-time since I became a mom.

So yes, you can make money as a freelancer. (Want to know more? My book, *Six-Figure Freelancing: The Writer's Guide to Making More Money* is aimed at experienced writers who want to boost their income without working eighty hours a week. That's been my business mantra for years.)

Get Over your Money Issues

If you are selling your work as a writer, you are writing for money. Don't be put off by the idea that **writing** = **money**. Ask any successful freelancer and I assure you, he or she has made peace with that idea. As a writer, you're providing a service—the ability to string a collection of specific words together in a specific order that will make your editor happy. Maybe it's several hundred words. Maybe it's several thousand. But whatever the project is, your ability to do it is what people will pay you for.

I'll be honest. I'm often annoyed by writers who won't cough up financial information when I ask, partly because I am open about what I make. As freelancers, we often labor in the dark, and knowing what other publishers pay or what other freelancers charge helps me in my business. And if you know what I make, that helps you, too, right?

No, not every writer is worth the same. A writer who makes only $12,000/year may be much more talented than a six-figure freelancer. (She may be smarter, sexier, and an all-around better person than her compatriot.) The money you make is only a reflection of the type of work you did that year, and the clients you did it for. That's it. It may not reflect how many hours you worked. It may not reflect your talent. It may not reflect your enthusiasm for your writing career. But it's a simple way for you (and others) to track your success.

In a bit, I'm going to talk about taxes, and what you need to know about them when you write for money. But before we do that, let's talk a little bit more about what to say when you're offered an assignment—for less money than you'd like.

As I mentioned last chapter, I use the TEA method, which stands for Thank, Explain, Ask. Let's say I'm offered an assignment to write a 500-word piece for an online market. In her email, the editor says she can pay $125 for all rights to the story. This isn't a terrible or unusually low rate for this kind of piece, but it's less than what I would like to be paid for it. So here are some examples of what I might say to her, either in an email or by phone:

"Thank you so much for offering me this assignment. I'm really excited to do this piece for you. [Thank.] You've offered me $125, and I know you need this piece by the end of the week. Considering that [Explain], could you pay me $250 instead? [Ask.]"

Not complicated at all, and I've given her a reason to say yes, and asked for more money in a professional way. I use the TEA method often, and while it doesn't always net me more money, I've never lost an assignment over it, either. (New writers sometimes worry that asking for more money will annoy an editor. I've never had that be the case. I have had plenty of editors say something along the lines of, "That's the best I can do—take it or leave it," and then it's up to me to decide whether to accept a story.)

Early in your freelance career, though, I suggest you take pretty much any reasonable assignment you're offered. No, I don't think you should write for a website that only pays, say $4 for a 1,000-word article. That's ridiculously low in my opinion. But if you're a new writer and you pitch a blog with some ideas, and the editor says she pays $50 for a 600-word post, I'd probably take the assignment. You're trying to gain clips (examples of your work, whether in print or online) and experience. As you get both, you're in a better position to pitch higher-paying markets and command higher rates as well. As a newbie with few or no clips, not so much.

Today, I ask myself four questions before I take on an assignment:

1. How much does it pay?
2. How much time will it take?
3. Will the assignment advance my career in some way, and if so, how?
4. What's the PIA factor? (PIA is a nice way of saying "Pain In The…" I think you can finish the phrase on your own.)

The questions you ask yourself before you take on an assignment may vary depending on where you are in your career, and I realize that. The first couple of years of fulltime freelancing, I took every assignment that was offered me. I'm not joking. I even wrote a couple of articles for free, thinking that the "exposure" would be worth, well, something. It wasn't.

This book is about writing for money, not about writing for nothing. So I suggest you always write for money, if it's only a little bit starting out. Start small, if necessary, and go from there.

The second question, how long will it take, isn't always apparent from the outset, but often you have a general idea of what's expected. If I take on a 1,300-word article for a parenting magazine I write for, I know it's going to require some background research and probably three to four interviews (two experts and two "real people" sources). [See chapter 8 for more on how many sources you need for stories of different lengths.]

I've written for my editor before and have a solid idea of what she'd be looking for, so it's unlikely that I'll need to rewrite the piece. I also know that she buys first N.A. serial and electronic rights, so I'm able to resell the story after it first comes out. [More about reselling work in chapter 12.] That's not a huge factor in whether I decide to take an assignment, but I do consider it.

Will this particular story advance my career? Not really. But I know the PIA factor is pretty much nonexistent. So I say yes to a market that pays $350, figuring it's about three to four hours' worth of work with few to no headaches involved.

Now let's say I've pitched a piece on how to keep your heart healthy, a story I recently covered. But in this case, my editor asks me to interview at least six leading cardiac medicine experts from throughout the country for the story. And include two more sidebars. And she wants me to turn around the story in eight days. And …well, you get the idea. The more work a story is going to take, the less likely I am to say "yes" to it unless I'm paid more to do it. I've done long, complicated stories that involved interviewing a dozen sources (and doing multiple rewrites!) for national magazines.

And been paid thousands of dollars for them. I sure wouldn't do that amount of work for, say, $500.

Maybe you want to set your "bottom dollar" figure for articles, or maybe you'll take anything that's offered for the first year of your career and then reevaluate. That's your call. In my opinion, though, every assignment you take should put something in your checking account, even if it's only enough for a cheap dinner out.

One last piece of advice about asking for more. It's tough to do the first few times, and maybe you want to do what I did. I worked as a freelancer for more than a year before I got up the nerve to ask for more money. By then, I was ready—and the first time I asked for more money from a market I'd worked for before, I got a boost from $0.50/word to $0.75/word! Not bad for opening my mouth. On other occasions, I've asked for more and been told no. I just did this with one of my regular clients, and my editor said, "I'm sorry, Kelly. You're already getting our top rate."

Well, the value of my relationship with my editor far exceeds me trying to squeeze a few extra bucks out of her. So I said, "No problem. You know how much I love working for you, but I figure it never hurts to ask." That way, I retain the relationship without appearing ungrateful (which believe me, I'm not!).

Talking Taxes

If this were a book on writing, I wouldn't have to address taxes. But it's about **writing for money**, so we must include the impact your writing income (and you will have income, if you adopt the strategies in these pages!) will have on your taxes.

As an American, every penny you make is considered taxable income as far as the federal government (and your state, and possibly your city or county) goes. But when you write for money (what the Internal Revenue Services calls that "having a profit motive"), as opposed to writing only for the pleasure or joy of it, you are allowed to deduct legitimate business expenses from your overall income.

I am not suggesting that the following discussion is any substitute for the advice of an accountant. But it will give you an idea of what you can expect to deduct from your gross income as a writer. And even if you only make a little bit of money—like several hundred or thousand dollars a year, I suggest you track your expenses. My first year of fulltime, I grossed just over $17,100 but my business expenses brought my net income down to about $11,400. (I had significant business expenses my first year which included the purchase of a computer and other office peripherals.) That meant I paid federal and state income tax and self-employment tax (I was a fulltime freelancer) on that amount instead of $17,100. Does that make it worth it to keep accurate records? You bet.

I think an example will help make this clear. Let's say you love oil painting. Between the cost of canvases, paints, brushes, classes and art books (hey, you need to study the masters' work in detail!), you shell out a good $3,700 one year.

You decide to call yourself a "professional" painter so you can write off that $3,700 as business expenses. After all, your neighbor, who displays her work at art shows, does the same thing, so no problem, right?

Hold on a minute. The government doesn't want hobbyists to be able to deduct the costs of their supplies and classes, and reduce the amount of money they pay tax on. So you have to be able to show you're operating a business, not a hobby, to be able to take advantage of having a business, and the primary factor the government looks at is the presence of a "profit motive."

Having a profit motive doesn't mean you have to make a profit your first year, or even your first few years. Plenty of businesses operate in the red when they open, or occasionally thereafter. So let's go back to the oil painting example. Let's say that you painted several dozen landscapes this year, and have given several away as gifts. That's it. Do you have a profit motive? I would say no, and I think the IRS would agree with me.

Now let's say you've painted several dozen landscapes this year. You have a Website where you offer your paintings for sale. You participate in art shows. You market yourself online and in person. You keep track of your painting-related expenses. As of this year, you haven't sold a painting, but I would argue that you have a profit motive. And I think the IRS would agree with me here too.

When you're writing for money, and have a profit motive, the IRS allows you to deduct "all ordinary, necessary, and reasonable expenses" that are incurred as you run your business. For writers, those expenses typically include:

- Computer (doesn't matter if you're a PC or a Mac!) and other office peripherals like a scanner/copier/fax machine;
- Office supplies like paper, printer cartridges, business cards, pens, highlighters, and thank-you notes;
- Postage/mailing costs;
- Membership fees to professional and writing-related organizations;
- Office equipment—e.g., desk, office chair, and file cabinets;
- Travel and entertainment related to your business (for example, flying to interview key sources or taking a client out to lunch. However, while you can deduct all of your work-related travel expenses, you can only take 50 percent of meals/entertainment costs);
- Internet access, website hosting, and other online fees;
- Telephone expenses (you can't deduct the expense of your primary phone line, but you can deduct long-distance charges related to your business as well as the cost of a second phone line and/or cell phone solely used for business); and
- Car expenses. The majority of self-employed writers use the standard mileage deduction, which will be $0.565/mile in 2013.

In addition, if you're self-employed, you may be able to deduct the cost of medical insurance premiums for yourself, your spouse, and your family. You may also be able to take a home office deduction if you work from home and use a section of it (be it a room or part of a room) *solely and exclusively* as your place of business. (Don't worry—you can still work at your local coffee shop for a change of scene. I'm a regular at my favorite Caribou. But most of your work should be done from your home office, and you shouldn't be doing anything non-work-related there either.)

I'm not a tax professional (hey, I'm not even a lawyer anymore), so if you have questions, talk to an accountant or visit www.IRS.gov for more info. (The *Tax Guide for Small Business*, Publication 334, is especially helpful.) Track all of your writing-related expenses and keep your receipts so in the rare event you're audited, you have proof of what you spent on your business, when, and why.

When I talk to new writers about their freelance income and taxes, a few of the same questions come up frequently:

Q: I'm a new writer and haven't sold anything yet. Should I still track my expenses?

A: Yes. You never know when you'll start selling your work, and once you do, every dollar you make is taxable. Keeping track of your freelance-writing expenses will reduce your overall tax liability. It's also proof that you consider your writing a business, not only a hobby. You may also be able to deduct your business expenses from your overall income, but talk to you accountant about that first.

Q: I was paid $450 by a magazine last year, but I didn't receive a 1099 from it. Do I still have to report the income?

A: Yup. While businesses only have to file 1099s for vendors they paid $600 and up during any given year, that doesn't exclude the payment from being considered income to you. To be on the safe side, report all of your freelance income, not only the money you receive 1099s from.

Q: I've spent money this year on books (like this one!) about freelancing. Can I deduct their cost?

A: Sure thing. I'd consider that a reasonable, ordinary, and necessary expense. Just keep in mind that your business expenses must be *reasonable*. So, for example, if you've only made a few hundred dollars as a freelancer and try to write off a $3,500 cruise where you take a memoir-writing class, the IRS may look at you askance—and disallow those deductions.

Q: What kind of mileage deductions can I take?

A: If you use the standard mileage deduction, which in 2013 will be $0.565/mile, you can deduct trips you make related to freelancing. I keep my mileage log as part of my daily calendar and write in it where I went, what the purpose of the trip was, and how many miles I traveled. I write off trips to the library to do background research, travel I do for speaking gigs, and travel to interview sources on the rare occasions I do an in-person interview as well as travel I undertake to meet an editor or potential client. Remember that you can also take travel-related expenses like tolls and parking fees.

Q: What if I have to travel further that that? Can I write that off?

A: Now it gets a little tricky. Let's say you decide to attend the annual conference put on by ASJA, the American Society of Journalists and Authors, in Manhattan each spring. You decide to stay an couple of extra days to sightsee. In this case, you'd be allowed to deduct the cost of your flight to NYC, the cost of the conference, and several days of hotel and meal expenses. However, you wouldn't be able to deduct anything for the days you were in NYC purely to sightsee. And keep the reasonable standard in mind—if I were a new writer with little or no income, I don't think I'd try to write off an expensive weekly writer's conference in Hawaii. On the other hand, with sixteen years of self-employment under my belt, the IRS would hopefully say that was a reasonable expense for *me*.

Q: What else can I do to help ensure that if I do get audited, the IRS considers me a business, not a hobby?

A: First, take your writing seriously. Set goals. Make time for your freelance career. Stick with it. Someone who attempts to sell her work and then abandons her efforts for months at a time doesn't appear to have a profit motive. Second, keep records—of what markets you've submitted to, of what expenses you've incurred, of what assignments you've received. Third (and this may seem obvious), submit to markets that pay! That's one of the clearest ways to show that you have the goal of making money since you started.

And if you do happen to get audited (knock on wood!), don't forget to show the auditor this book as evidence you're writing for money!

CHAPTER 7

The Process, Demystified: How to Pitch, Research, and Write Short Articles

So, now you're familiar with the basic concepts of freelancing. You know how to come up with ideas for stories, how to write queries, and what to look for in a contract. The next step is actually writing a piece, and this is where you may flounder.

When writing any article, regardless of market, topic, format, or length, I tell freelancers to keep two questions in mind:

1. **Who am I writing for?** (Who are the readers of this publication? What do they care about? What are they interested in? Why do they read this particular print or online market or blog?); and
2. **What do they need to know about this subject?** (What is surprising/important/interesting/significant about your topic? In other words, why will readers **care** about your story?)

That's it. Keep those two questions in mind and you're halfway there.

Okay, I lied. It's not *quite* that easy. Before you sit down to write an article, you have to research, pitch, and sell it—and then probably conduct more research. Then you write the piece itself.

In short, to pitch, sell, research, and write an article, you'll do the following:

1. Come up with an idea. (This is unnecessary if an editor approaches you with an assignment.)
2. Choose the market for your idea. (You may already be pitching and/or writing for a market that you plan to pitch. Otherwise, you'll need to find the market you plan to approach with your idea. And it never hurts to have more than one potential market in mind—that way, if an editor says "no," you move on and resub the idea to another market, remember?)
3. Research and write a query letter, and send it to your target market.

4. Send a follow-up, if you haven't heard from the target market yet. *in 4 weeks / resend*
5. If you get a rejection (what I call a "bong"), return to step 2 and resub to another market. If the article is assigned by an editor, ask about the publication's contract terms (see step 6), and prepare to research and write the piece.
6. Read your contract, and negotiate any writer-unfriendly terms as best you can. [See chapter 5.]
7. Research the piece. This may include doing background research, identifying and contacting potential sources, and conducting interviews with sources.
8. Write the piece, doing your best to meet your editor's specifications—in other words, give her what she wants.
9. Turn the piece in and wait for feedback from your editor.
10. Rewrite or rework the piece if necessary, and submit backup, or fact-checking material, if she requests it. (Some markets require it; others do not.)
11. Submit an invoice, if your editor needs one. Otherwise, she'll request payment on your behalf.
12. Wait for the piece to appear in print or online, and notify your sources that the story is out.
13. Collect your check!
14. Celebrate seeing your byline in print—and move on to the next story idea, with a little more confidence and experience under your belt.

You won't necessarily perform every step for every story, but this process gives you an idea of what to expect when you write for publication. But maybe you're thinking, it can't be that easy! How do I find experts? What do I say when I contact one? How do I pull a story together? How do I know I'm doing a good job?

When I teach magazine writing, I've found that the best way to teach these skills is by showing students how I've approached stories in the past. So in this chapter, we'll look at some short articles, and how I pitched, researched, and wrote them—and you'll learn how to do the same thing as a new freelancer. Consider it a speed-dating approach to article writing.

We'll start with some simple, short pieces (as a new writer, you're more likely to get these kinds of short assignments) and then in the next chapter, we'll move on to more complex articles.

The Short Article

Recall that to get your foot in the door as a new freelancer, you'll have more success pitching short pieces for the FOB ("front of book") sections of a publication. Even if you're writing for an online publication, I suggest you start with shorter pieces. An editor is more likely to take a chance on a new writer for a short piece. First, it's easier to report and write a short piece compared to a longer story. If you can write a compelling query for a short piece, your work is more than half done—in many cases, your query may wind up being longer than the actual story!

So you're probably thinking, why not just write the piece and send it in, instead of bothering with a query? Well, first off, you want to make the best impression possible, and professional freelancers send query letters, even for short pieces. We don't just write something, send it in, and pray, remember?

So, sending a query lets an editor know that you understand the rules of the game. Second, even a short piece may not be what your editor is looking for in terms of subject matter, angle, types of sources, format, you name it. So pitching a piece lets your editor consider your approach and then decide whether it appeals to him.

Let's take a look at the process of writing a simple one-source story.

Step 1: Come up with an idea.

As a long-term runner, I've been interested in fitness topics for years. The idea for this particular story came about after I came across a press release about a new study about something called "non-exercise activity," or NEAT. Researchers at the Mayo Clinic found that NEAT (things like fidgeting, shifting position, jiggling your leg during a boring meeting) may burn more calories than originally thought, and may help people maintain a healthy weight. It was surprising to me, and made a good "hook" for a pitch.

However, simply reading the press release didn't give me enough detail to write a strong query. So I went online to search PubMed.gov, the U.S. National Library of Medicine's database of more than 22 million journal articles. There I pulled up the abstract to the article itself. (An abstract is a brief summary of a journal article; it includes the citation, title study, authors' names, and background and a short overview of the study results. If you've never used PubMed before, www.ncbi.nlm.nih.gov/books/NBK3827/ gives a great overview with tips about how to search it.)

In this case, the article had been published in the December, 2000 edition of the *American Journal of Clinical Nutrition*. Though it was a small study (involving only 24 participants), the conclusion stated, "There is marked variance between subjects in the energy expenditure associated with self-selected fidgeting-like activities. The thermogenic [calorie-burning] potential of fidgeting-like and low-grade activities is sufficiently great to substantively contribute to energy balance." (Yeah, that's awkward phrasing. But the researcher wrote it, not me!)

With the abstract in hand, I could write a query letter. In the meantime, I requested a copy of the article through my local library. (Your library is often able to obtain copies of journal articles for little or no charge; this is less expensive than using a source like LexisNexis, www.lexisnexis.com, or Electric Library, www.elibrary.com, both of which you must pay to use.) Many libraries and universities allow you to access the full-text articles in their research databases for no charge; check out Stanford University's High Wire Press, which includes more than two million full-text science and health articles (www.highwire.stanford.edu/lists/freeart.dtl) or New York Public Library's collections at http://www.nypl.org/collections.

Back to my article. At this point, I didn't bother to contact one of the study authors. I typically wait until the story is assigned to do that. (The only exception I make to this rule is if I know I'll need to interview a particular person for the story, such as with a profile. Then I contact that person first to make sure he is available and willing to speak with me if and when I get the assignment. That way I feel confident that I can deliver the story if it's assigned.)

Step 2: Choose the market.

Now that I had my story idea, and had started my background research, I had to figure out where I could sell the story. In this case, I decided *Fitness*, a market aimed at fitness-conscious women in their 20s and 30s, would be a perfect fit, so I pitched it there first. In chapter 2, you learned about the different types of markets and how to locate potential ones.

I like to start with my "first choice" market (usually the market that pays the most, or that I've written for before), but I keep a list of other possible markets in the event my first choice says no. If that happens, I move on and resub the query to another market.

It's easier than ever before to analyze a potential market; most print and online magazines now have their writers' guidelines posted online. This is no substitute for actually reading the publication you hope to write for, however.

Review your target market with a critical eye. What subjects does it cover? What types of articles (i.e., features, profiles, service, and short pieces) does it include? How long are the articles? How many articles does a typical issue feature? Do the pieces rely on a lot of expert voices, "real" people (think anecdotal sources), or a combination of both? What kind of "tone" or voice does the market have?

Look at the ads, too; they will tell you more about the readers of both print and online publications. The more you know about the market, the more likely you are to pitch an idea that an editor will want to assign.

Step 3: Write a query.

Next up, the query letter. We talked about query letters in chapter 3. Remember that you want to capture the editor's attention; explain why her readers will be interested; describe how you plan to approach the story; and demonstrate that you're "uniquely qualified" (yup, there's that phrase again!) to write the piece.

Here's the query I wrote. It's relatively short and simple:

Dear Heather [I'd written for her before; otherwise I'd refer to her as Ms. or Mr. Last Name]:

Lead → You say your best friend can eat *anything* without gaining weight? Maybe it's because she can't sit still. [Brief but attention-getting lead.]

A recently published study conducted by the Mayo Clinic found that fidgeting may not just get your through a boring meeting—it may help you maintain a whittled waist, too. Sixteen volunteers were fed an extra 1,000 calories a day for eight weeks. While all of the volunteers gained weight, participants burned off about half of those calories each day due to increased non-exercise activity thermogenesis ("NEAT")—things like fidgeting and changing position. Yet some participants burned a lot more calories through NEAT than others, which means that fidgeting may actually help you lose weight. [Because I'm pitching such a short piece, I'm keeping the query itself short as well.] *why read?*

Interested in a short piece about this new research for "Fit Buzz?" I'll interview one of the study researchers for this informative piece, which will be about 200 words. [I've suggested the section of the magazine I think this story will fit in. This also lets the editor know I'm familiar with her publication. And I suggested a length of 200 words because the guidelines said the section uses pieces up to 200 words. I suggest you always include possible word count as another way of demonstrating market familiarity.] *nuts & bolts*

As you know, I'm a freelance writer who's written for *Fitness* before, and believe your readers will enjoy this piece. Please let me know if you have any questions about the story. [I had a relationship with this editor already so my ISG doesn't have to be that strong. If not, I would have written the best ISG I could, mentioning my long-time interest in fitness and nutrition, for example. The very fact that I came up with this idea on my own makes me somewhat uniquely qualified, too. At least I think so!]

Thank you very much for your time; I look forward to hearing from you soon.

Very truly yours,
Kelly James-Enger

If I hadn't worked with Heather before, I would have confirmed the name of the editor who was in charge of the "Fit Buzz" section by calling *Fitness* and asking for her name and email address. (Today, you may be able to find this information from the publication's Website. Otherwise, call or email to make sure that you're contacting the appropriate person.) Then I proofread the query, and emailed it.

Step 4: Get the assignment.

In this case, I didn't need to send a follow-up email. Just two weeks later, the editor called to assign the piece. She asked me to keep it to 150 words, and we agreed on a rate of $1.50/word for the story. I'd written for *Fitness* before, so I was familiar with the magazine's multi-page contract. Otherwise, I would have wanted to read the contract and make sure I was comfortable with its terms before proceeding. [See chapter 5 for more contract advice.]

Step 5: Contact my source.

Recall that while I already had a copy of the abstract, I'd also requested a full-length copy of the article through my library. I had the study, but wanted to interview one of the study authors for the article. The study listed the name and email address of the person to contact at Mayo Clinic with questions, which made my job easy. I sent the following email:

> Dear Sir or Madam:
>
> I'm a freelancer writing a short piece for *Fitness* magazine about the recently published study on NEAT. Could you arrange a brief phone interview with one of the study authors for me? I'm on deadline and would like to speak to someone in the next week if possible; I'm of course happy to work around the researcher's schedule.
>
> Thank you very much, and I look forward to hearing from you!
> Kelly James-Enger
> Freelancer writer/journalist

The contact person arranged for me to speak with Michael Jensen, PhD, one of the study authors, a few days later. I made a note of the date and time of the interview, the phone number I was to reach him at, and then called him at the appointed time.

But let's say that I didn't have access to this study, or wasn't sure who I should interview for the story. How would I research the topic then?

First, if I know next to nothing about a subject, I'll often check Wikipedia. com for some background on it. This doesn't "count" as research but it helps you get up to speed as a writer so you can determine your next step. After I know what I'm writing about (or at least have a general clue), I identify potential sources.

Often finding the appropriate "expert" (as opposed to an anecdotal, or "real person" source) is all I need for a short piece as that expert provides me with the facts, stats, quotes, and background I need. You can use a number of methods to locate sources, including:

- Google. Google can be your best friend when it comes to locating potential sources. In this case, you might type search terms like "exercise physiology" and "association" or "organization" to see what groups come up. When you locate an appropriate-looking organization, contact the public relations or media department, introduce yourself, and ask if it can refer you to a possible source. You'll find that organizations can be extremely helpful in locating sources for writers and reporters.

- HARO, or Help a Reporter Out (www.helpareporterout.com), allows you to send a source request (e.g., "I'm looking for an exercise physiologist to interview about NEAT and its implications for weight loss") that is distributed to thousands of experts and PR pros.
- Profnet (www.media.prnewswire.com). Similar to HARO, but with a huge plus: you can search its database of experts to locate an expert. Or, like HARO, you can send what they call a "query" specifying what you're looking for in a source.
- Amazon. Look for books on the subject, and then check out their authors. I suggest you look for an established expert—someone with an advanced degree, a connection to a university or college and/or at least a decade of experience—to interview.
- Universities. Start with large, established universities, and search their websites for experts in your subject area. Or, as with an organization, go directly to its media relations page and ask for help. The people there will be able to hook you up with an appropriate professor, researcher, or other faculty member to interview.

Still stuck? Don't forget my magic weapon—your local library's reference desk. Call or email and explain what you're looking for, and what (if any) steps you've taken so far to locate the person, fact, or statistic. Chances are they'll be able to help you. (Live in a small town? Then reach out to a library in a larger city and go from there. And don't forget to send a thank-you note if the person is particularly helpful! You'll make your librarian's day.)

Step 6: Conduct my interview.

Back to our current assignment. To make sure I wouldn't forget any relevant questions, I wrote them down beforehand. Here's my list:

- Confirm name and title
- Mailing address (so I can send him a thank-you note after the interview)/email address
- Explain research findings briefly
- Was he surprised by this? Why or why not?
- Take-away message for women who want to lose/maintain their weight?
- Anything else you want to add that I haven't asked?

Questions in hand, I called Dr. Jensen at the time we'd agreed. The first question I asked him was, "Is this still a good time for you to talk?" That shows respect for his time, and if he needs to push back the time, I can accommodate him. Then I asked permission to record the interview (I use a digital recorder that hooks into my phone jack); in some states, it's illegal to record without the subject's permission. (You don't have to record interviews, but it makes it easier to quote your sources accurately, especially if they turn out to be fast talkers. Check out Hello Direct, www.hellodirect.com, for headsets and digital recorders. On the other hand, if you take notes quickly, you may not need to record your interviews.)

At the conclusion of the interview, I thanked Dr. Jensen for his time, and told him I'd be in touch with any further questions via email. I also asked whether he'd be available in the next month or two in case my editor had any follow-up questions. Finally, I promised him I'd be in touch to let him know when the story was published. And then I sent him a thank-you note via snail mail, expressing appreciation for his time.

Scared about conducting an interview? I used to be, too. In fact, I'd say I was petrified I'd forget to ask something, or that I'd sound stupid (or both!) during pretty much every interview I conducted for the first year or two of freelancing. But I'll tell you something—the person you're interviewing doesn't care about you sounding stupid—he's more concerned about whether *he* sounds stupid.

Keeping that in mind, I'd like to give you some tips to get better interviews, regardless of who you're speaking with. First, always do your homework ahead of time. Second, let your source know that you have. I've interviewed hundreds of experts and real people over the years, many of whom are busy professionals. They may be willing to be interviewing, but that doesn't mean they're eager to be. As soon as I make sure that it's still a good time for the person to speak with me, I demonstrate that I'm prepared to speak with him.

So, for example, with Dr. Jensen, I told him that I'd already read the entire journal article, but wanted some "live" quotes from him for the story. With another source, I might let him know that I'd visited his Website or mention one of his books or some of his latest research. It depends on the source and the subject, but even with an anecdotal source, I can say something like, "Becky, thanks so much for agreeing to speak with me. I understand from Sarah that you've been homeschooling your kids for three years, and I had a chance to check out your homeschooling blog. Is this still a good time for you?" It's that easy to start your interview off on a positive note.

I always tell the person I'm interviewing how much time I'll need (say, 15 minutes) and I stick to that estimate. Watch the clock. If the interview is going to go over, tell your source. "I'll say something like, 'You know, I told you I only needed 15 minutes to speak with you, but we're about to hit that. Can we speak for a few minutes, please?" It's another way of doing what you said you would, and demonstrating your professionalism.

Finally, I always send a thank-you note. I mentioned that already but I'll tell you that it's made a huge difference in my career. Sources remember me! They remember my name even years later because, "You're the one who sent that note!" People think of me as a professional, thoughtful writer—and there are much worse things to be known of in a business where your reputation may precede you.

For this story, I only needed a couple of brief quotes from Jensen, so the interview took less than five minutes. My transcript included Dr. Jensen's contact information and several short statements about the study. With the study and my transcript in hand, I sat down to write the story.

Step 7: Write the piece.

To write the piece, I considered two primary questions:

1. What made the study interesting or surprising?
2. What "take-away" message was there for *Fitness* readers?

Obviously this was a short article, so I didn't have a lot of space. This story was relatively easy to write, both because it was short, and because the subject matter was fairly simple. The challenge was "writing tight," or keeping my story succinct while adequately covering the topic. I kept my lead short, described the research, and included a quote from Dr. Jensen. It took me several drafts to get my original version, which was more than 250 words, cut to within word count. It had been assigned at 150 words and I wrote a 163-word piece. My rule of thumb is to get as close to word count as you can, but stay within 10 percent of assigned word count no matter what.

The finished piece I turned in is below. Note that my name, address and contact information are in the left-hand corner. The word count and rights being sold are included in the upper right-hand corner. Then the title of the piece and the byline are centered below that, before the story starts. You should single-space this information and double-space the piece itself.

Kelly James-Enger
[street address]
[city, state, zip]
[phone]
[email]

163 words
Rights per written contract

Fidgeting Fat Away?

by

Kelly James-Enger

Maybe those enviably skinny people who can eat *anything* without gaining weight simply can't sit still. [Very short lead—this is a very short piece, remember?]

Researchers at the Mayo Clinic's Endocrine Research Unit fed sixteen volunteers 1,000 extra calories a day for eight weeks while strictly monitoring their activities. While all participants gained weight, on average they burned off about half of those extra calories through increased non-exercise activity thermogenesis ("NEAT"), which includes fidgeting, maintaining posture, shifting position, and other spontaneous physical activities. The range varied significantly—participants whose NEAT kicked into high gear expended more calories and gained less weight while others—with smaller NEAT increases—expended fewer calories, putting on more weight. [Here's the heart of the piece—explaining what the study revealed.]

"It looks like NEAT can be dramatically and rapidly induced in some people by eating too much," says researcher Michael Jensen, Ph.D. We're not recommending fidgeting as a weight-loss technique, but the study suggests that even minor physical activities—like stretching when you're watching TV or crossing and uncrossing your legs during a marathon meeting—can add up. [Live quote from one of the researchers, and a short closing statement.]

-30-

[The number 30, or ###, indicates the end of the piece.]

Step 8: Turn the story in.

I turned in the story along with Dr. Jensen's contact information and a copy of the study itself. This is called "backup," or "fact-checking" material. Some publications don't require backup, but I suggest you always have it on hand just in case. That will include the names and contact information of anyone you interview; copies of journal articles; Websites that you pulled information from (e.g., a page from the Centers for Disease Control that you cite in the article.) For longer stories that include more than one source, you typically turn in an additional, annotated copy of the story that indicates which sources provided the information in the story. [You'll see an example of this in chapter 8.]

Step 9: Get paid!

In this case, my editor was happy with the piece, so I didn't need to do any revisions. She put payment through, and I received my check for $225 four weeks later.

Step 10: Get the clip and notify my sources.

Five months later, the piece ran in *Fitness*. I made a copy for my portfolio, and notified Dr. Jensen about the piece, thanking him again for his help. If it would have appeared in a trade or custom publication that's hard to locate, I would have sent him a copy of the article, but in this case, I simply told him the name and issue of the magazine, and the page number of the story (and his quote).

Get the idea? A short piece like this isn't complicated to pitch, research, and write—once you understand the steps to take.

Another Short Article

Let's take a look at another simple, one-source story that any new freelancer could write.

Step 1: Get the assignment.

In this case, I'd worked with the editor before. He asked me to write a short piece on forcing bulbs for a custom magazine for people with a certain medical condition. We agreed I'd be paid $0.75/word for the 300-word article.

Because the editor came to me, I didn't have to come up with an idea or write a query. That's the upside. The downside is that because I didn't come up with the idea, I was a bit clueless. I didn't even know what "forcing bulbs" meant! I also had to make sure I knew what he was looking for in terms of length, content, and angle. The story he had in mind was simple—a short how-to piece for a winter issue on getting flowers to bloom out of season.

The simplicity of this story makes it an idea any writer who had some gardening or plant experience could pitch. Then you'd pick a market for it, write your query, and resub it as necessary until you received an assignment.

Step 2: Research the piece.

Back to the story at hand. My first step was to do a little background research on "forcing bulbs" because I'm not a gardener. After getting up to speed on the subject (never underestimate the value of Wikipedia!), I needed to find an expert on the subject. I'm a member of the American Society of Journalists and Authors, so I checked our directory of members for an appropriate resource. I found that Julie Bawden Davis was a master gardener and the author of multiple books on plants, including *Houseplants and Indoor Houseplants*, and contacted her to see if she'd be willing to do an interview on forcing bulbs.

If I hadn't found Davis, I could have used other techniques to find an appropriate expert:

- Searched Google for the words "indoor plant" and "expert" (which produces a variety of gardening experts who would be potential sources);
- Searched Amazon for books on indoor gardening and considered the authors as potential experts. If I did this, I'd want to do some research on their bios and backgrounds to make sure they're qualified to serve as an expert for my piece. A hobby gardener who has self-published a book on tulips probably won't fit the bill but a Master gardener with a decade of experience probably will.

- Looked for an organization that could suggest an expert, such as the American Horticultural Society (I found this by putting the terms "horticulture" and "organization" into Google), and then contacted the organization. I'd ask for its public affairs or media affairs person, and then ask that the person suggest a qualified expert I could interview; or
- Contacted a major university or college, asked for its media affairs department, and asked for a horticultural expert to interview.

If you're not sure about what type of expert will work for a particular piece, don't be afraid to ask your editor. I'll say something like, "So, I'm thinking a professor of horticulture would work for this story—does that sound good?" to make sure the editor and I are on the same page.

When I contacted Davis to arrange the interview, I told her what the story was about so she could prepare in advance. I've found that I get much better interviews when I tell a source the types of questions I plan to ask ahead of time. Think about it. If I asked you to tell me the top five keys to a happy relationship, you'd be caught off-guard and I couldn't expect great quotes. If, however, I tell you that I'll be asking you that question when we talk tomorrow at 3:00 p.m. Eastern Central Time, you'll have had a chance to think about the subject. You'll give me a better interview, which means I'll have better quality material to write a better piece. Get the idea?

Another thing—I prefer to conduct interviews by phone rather than by email. First off, when you ask to interview someone via email, you're asking them to do part of your job—namely, type up the answers to *your* questions. Second, phone interviews are more immediate, and allow you to pursue a line of questioning based on your subject's answer in a way that email doesn't. Third, I've found that email interviews tend to sound a little "canned."

That being said, I now do offer a source the opportunity to do the interview via email if that's her preference. I make it clear that *I* prefer to speak by phone, but if email works better for my source, I'll accommodate her. About 80 percent of the time, the person prefers to speak by phone. (Unless you write for a local paper, in-person interviews are rare. Expect to conduct 99 percent of yours via email and phone.)

While I transcribe notes during an interview, I almost always record it too, assuming I have permission from my source. That makes it easy to go back and fill in any missing information if my subject talks too quickly, I type too slowly, or both.

You'll find that when you interview people, they rarely speak in complete sentences or use perfect grammar. That's okay—you can always punctuate your quotes when you pull them out to use them in an article. Here's the actual transcript of the interview, with my questions in brackets:

Julie Bawden Davis
[phone number, mailing address, and email have been omitted]

[Tell me the name of your most recent book on plants]
Houseplants and Indoor Houseplants (Black and Decker Outdoor Series)

Q [What does "forcing bulbs" mean?]
A it's basically what you're doing is tricking them into blooming, into flowering out of season, on your timetable, generally a lot of these are spring bulbs, usually doing spring bulbs and what you're doing is tricking them over winter to flower indoors, whereas when you have a bulb normally speaking, it would be chilling and building up its reserves over the winter, so in the spring it would be ready to bloom, so you're mimicking the situation the winter going into spring indoors and that forces the bulb to flower

Q [What types of bulbs are the easiest to force?]
A the best of all of them, especially for the beginner, is the paper white narcissus , it's really neat, as long as you like the smell, some people find it too overwhelming, that's by far the easiest and that's almost foolproof

Other ones are hyacinth, amaryllis, and then some that may do OK are some varieties of crocus and some tulips and the Chinese sacred lily, Narcissus tazetta, there's also another one, the iris, Iris danforviae, iris reticulate [note that I may not be spelling all of these flower names correctly, but I can double-check them if I include them in the article]

[So how do you force bulbs]
Two different ways to do this, one is regular potting soil, plant them with the top third of the bulb sticking out of the soil and then, keep the soil moist, or can do them in water, take a decorative see-through bowl and none of them would have drainage holes, a vase or container works well and put in marbles or decorative pebbles, do the same thing, expose the top third of the bulb and fill it up with water...right to the a little bit under that, the roots will go down and seek the water. Leave 1/3 to ½ inch between bulb and water, keep the container in a dark area to simulate the winter weather, good areas, basements, closet and garage if it isn't opening and closing constantly, should be fairly dark, and then you want to keep it the bulb 1/3 showing, water it well when you first plant it, you want it dampened but not soggy, that's where they're going to form their root structure,

When they have 4 to 6 inches growth on them or when the roots have filled the base, remove them and place them in a dimly lit area for about a week, the corner of a room that doesn't get a ton of light, for a bout a week, and then move to a medium light location, what's going to happen is the roots will grow and the top will start to sprout, dimly lit for a week, , and the medium lit for a week and at that point they'll start budding up, during this whole procedure they should be greening they should be white green at first, then lime green and then dark green, and in the last stage, then you put them in their final destination, which is a bright area, forced bulbs will flower anywhere from 4 to 16 weeks after planting depending on the flower, narcissus are on the shorter end of it

[When can readers find bulbs? Advice about buying them?]
buy them in Sep, as soon as possible, you want to get the best selection, larger the bulb the better, very firm and not rotted, some bulbs do need to be pre-chilled, crocus and narcissus, and hyacinth do need to be pre-chilled, paper whites don't need that, pre-chill average temperature, most fridges would be fine, store them in a paper bag or a plastic net bag so there's air moving through it, but the really important thing is to keep them away fruit such as apples, which releases ethylene gas, which will cause them to rot,

[How long will the flowers last?] paper whites will last about two to three weeks, hyacinths 2 to 4 weeks, depends on the atmosphere in your house, if the heat is on a lot, keep them away from heating vents and drafts,
depends on the type but in general they'll last two to three weeks

[How much should readers expect to spend?]
get them cheaper anywhere from $1/bulb especially at the height of the season, $3/bulb, bag at Home Depot but they don't always have a good selection, the nurseries have the best

[How much do you need to water them?] Watering when they are approaching dryness, because they are in the growth cycle, but don't overwater and there's no need to fertilize them because they store their own food, you might have to stake them, the brighter the light are, staking them, they always say the brighter the light they're in, but by the time, stake them the foliage itself can get a good one a half feet tall, it doesn't stand up, have a stake, once it gets to six inches, stake it

[Anything else to add?]
For water forcing best ones are crocus hyacinth and narcissus, and the hyacinth jars which are hourglass shaped jars, the water goes to the part, you would put the water to right below where the, hyacinth but you can use those for paperweights

Buy and stagger them, buy quite a few and the bulbs that don't go in... store in a mesh bag, cool dry dark place, fairly dark place can be hung up, in that area, moisture is their enemy and light will make them sprout

Step 3: Write the piece.
Thanks to my comprehensive interview with Davis, I had plenty of

material for this story. In fact, a quick review of my transcript reveals that I have about 900 words of notes for a piece that is supposed to be 300 words. Yikes! But my job is to take the information I've learned and turn it into a short "how-to" piece. To do so, I considered what readers would need to know about forcing bulbs, and kept the story focused on that.

I also decided to use subheads to organize the material. While I included Davis' name and book title, I didn't use any direct quotes as I felt the story flowed better without them. Here's the finished piece I turned in, along with Davis' contact information for fact-checking:

Kelly James-Enger   326 words
[contact info]   Rights per written contract

Welcome Spring Early:
How to Force Bulbs

by

Kelly James-Enger

Want to perk up your winter? Fill your home with the scent and beauty of fresh flowers by forcing bulbs. "Forcing" bulbs means tricking them into blooming early by mimicking seasonal change indoors, explains master gardener Julie Bawden Davis, author of *Houseplants and Indoor Houseplants*. [Brief lead that also introduces my expert.]

Buy the Best Bulbs

To get the best selection, buy bulbs during September. Look for large, firm bulbs that have no signs of rot; they'll cost $1 to $3 each. At home, store the bulbs in a cool, dry, dark place. Some bulbs, including crocus, iris, and hyacinth, need to be pre-chilled by keeping them in the refrigerator or other cool place for 12-14 weeks before forcing them. Paper white narcissus, one of the easiest bulbs to force, requires no pre-chilling. [Tells readers how to buy bulbs and which types to choose.]

Plant, Wait and Watch

You can force bulbs in water or soil. To use soil, plant the bulb in potting soil, leaving the top third exposed. The soil should be kept damp but not soggy. To use water, place pebbles or marbles at the bottom of a container, place the bulb on top, and then fill with water, leaving about ¼ inch between the water and the bottom of the bulb. (The roots will grow down, seeking the water.)

Place the bulb in a dark area like a basement or closet. It will form its root structure in a week or two. When its roots are four to six inches long or have filled the container base, place the container in a dimly lit area for about a week. Then, move the bulb to a medium light location to mimic spring's longer days. The top will start to sprout, and buds will appear. As the top begins to sprout, stake the foliage when it reaches about six inches. [Explains how to force bulbs.]

Place the bulb in a bright area to enjoy its blooms, and keep it away from drafts and heating vents. The blossoms will last for two to four weeks, depending on the flower. [Simple closing, though I could have certainly chosen something more flowery, pardon the pun.]

-30-

Step 4: Turn in the piece.
My editor was happy with the story, and I didn't have to do anything else other than turn over Davis' contact information for fact-checking. (Smaller magazines and websites may not fact-check, but always assume that your editor may need your backup, and be willing and able to provide it.)

Step 5: Get paid.
I received my check for $225 about four weeks later.

Step 6: Get the clip and notify my source.
When the story ran in a custom publication three months later, I sent Davis a copy of it, thanking her again for her time. I haven't written about bulbs, flowers, or gardening since then, but if I do in the future, I'll want to use her as a source. Thanking her for her help and letting her know about the story's publication will ensure she remembers me.

A Two-Source Short Piece
While I tend to use one source for a short article, your editor may ask you to interview more than one person for even a brief story. Here's an example:

Step 1: Get the assignment.
An editor I'd worked with contacted me to ask me to do a short article

based on a new study that had found that school-aged children tended to gain weight during the summer. In addition to talking about the study, she wanted to offer readers ways to combat this potential problem as well. That's why she suggested I interview two sources for the story. I had written for this market, so I didn't worry about the contract and could immediately start researching the piece. She offered me $1.50/word for 250 words, which I accepted.

Step 2: Locate and interview my sources.

I ordered a copy of the complete journal article through my local library and contacted the lead author, Paul von Hippel, PhD, to set up an interview. Then I contacted the American Dietetic Association to ask for a referral to a registered dietitian who was an ADA spokesperson. Often large organizations have lists of spokespeople, or experts in certain areas, who are experienced media pros and make for good interviews. I spoke with both sources for about ten minutes each; their transcripts appear below, with my questions in brackets.

Paul t. von Hippel, PhD, lead study author and statistician at Ohio State University [contact info deleted]

[What led to this study?]

It was the question, Doug Downey's idea, whether schools are really to blame for childhood obesity a lot of the public policy focus is on public schools and what they might be doing to exacerbate the problem and here was a unique opportunity for us to look at how quickly kids gain weight when they're in school and when they're not and what we found that schools are part of the solution, not part of the problem, kids would be a lot heavier if they weren't in school

[How was the study conducted?]

The study was done by the department of education, and not a lot of detail about how kids are spending their time but our feeling is that the structure of the school day restricts kids from the opportunity to eat and schedules regular time for exercise, right now it's 2:35 on a Monday pretty much be guaranteed that every kid in school isn't eating right now where in the summer, who knows that they would be doing

[Can you comment on the study results?]

The study shifts the focus from what schools are doing wrong to what schools are doing right and what we can learn from them. What they're doing right is providing children with some kind of structure, when it comes to summer, that you're providing some kind of structure, if you're home you can make sure they get to the park, make sure they're not wandering into the pantry every time they're bored and if you're not home or are but don't want to spend all your time with your kids, alternatives day camp or overnight camp

Amy Jamieson-Petonic
RD, spokesperson for the American Dietetic Association
Cleveland Clinic, manager, employee wellness program

[contact info deleted]
[Do you think kids eat better during the school year? Why?]

I agree, I think kids really do benefit by having structure, to all of a sudden you put them into a free-for-all I think kids do better with a specific timetable, knowing this is when breakfast is and this is when lunch is and even having set times for that and having set activities, and other thing is for kids who have absolutely no structure in the summer, they really have a hard time getting back to bed at a normal time and getting back into the swing of things when school starts, so it's really more difficult for these kids to get acclimated when the summer's over, so really try to maintain that structure over the summer with specific mealtimes, specific snack times, not kind of this roving and eating whenever you want

[Suggestions for parents?]

I have a whole list here. The most important tip is to be involved, and include your kids in ways to develop and maintain a healthy lifestyle.

Plan for daily physical activity: Games, activities such as swimming, baseball, tag, bike riding or anything else that keeps them moving is great. We have wonderful parks here that have trails as well as paved paths for nature hikes, bike rides, walking, roller blading, and open space for Frisbee or any other activity you could imagine.

Take a vacation or day trip that involves physical activity: A family bike ride, a visit to a national park, a camping trip, or staying at places with a pool all find ways to include active living into the day.

Limit the TV or computer time: During the summer months, there is increased availability of "screen" time, which may replace physical activity.

Play an active role in fostering a healthy lifestyle. For example, there are a number of ways that parents can role models in living healthy. Here are just a few:

Plant a garden: what a great activity for families to do together! You can learn about fruits and vegetables by planting them, tending to them, and eating them when they are ready. Growing tomatoes, green peppers, cauliflower, and berries can be a great way for families to learn about foods and spent time together.

Go strawberry picking. In Ohio, the first few weeks of June are strawberry picking time. I encourage parents and kids to go out and pick berries, which can be educational in it, take them home, clean them, and prepare a number of dishes with them. Fresh strawberries with fat free whipped cream is a fun and yummy treat.

Go to a farmer's market. Parents can teach their kids where different foods come from, and have the opportunity to meet and talk to the farmers that grow it. Summer produce is full of vitamins and minerals, and can give kids another perspective on how food is made.

Out of sight, out of mind: If parents have high fiber, low fat foods in the house, that's what the kids will eat. Be proactive about planning for set meal times and set snack times to prevent too much snacking or grazing all day long. There is nothing wrong with an occasional treat, but the majority of foods kids consume should be nutrient dense. Even helping them make less calorically dense foods will help. For example, if ice cream is what they would like: provide a lower fat version and put fresh fruit or a handful of nuts on it. This will provide additional vitamins and minerals, as well as heart healthy fats with the nuts.

Go to the grocery store together and ask the kids to choose one new fruit or vegetable no one has tried, and prepare it for a meal. Once again, this gets the whole family involved in healthy living activities.

As for the unstructured time: once again, sit down with your kids and develop a plan of what they would like to do over the summer, including healthy living activities, and help them stick with it. Let them know that summer can be a great time, but helping your kids learn about balance, variety and moderation will help them for years to come.

Wondering why Jamieson-Petonic had such specific, info-laden answers? Two reasons. Number one, she's a spokesperson so she's used to doing interviews. Second, I told her in advance that I would ask her for suggestions for parents to help their kids maintain a healthy weight during the summer. By telling her what I would ask, she was able to prepare in advance and give me a great interview. You'll see, below, how much of her answers I wound up using.

Step 4: Write the piece.

As you can see, I had more than enough for a 250-word story. The real challenge here was "writing tight," especially when I had so many great tips from my dietitian source for the piece. Here's the finished piece, with my comments in brackets:

Kelly James-Enger				278 words
[Contact info]					Rights per written contract

Does Summer Boost Snacking?

Study Finds Kids More Likely to Gain Weight Out of School

by

Kelly James-Enger

Think schools are making kids fat? Think again, according to a new study in the *American Journal of Public Health*. [Newsy lead to catch readers' attention.]

Researchers compared the BMI, or body mass index, of more than five thousand children at the beginning and end of kindergarten and first grade. They found that the average BMI growth per month was more than twice as fast during summer months than during the school year. [Summary of the study results.]

"We found that schools are part of the solution, not part of the problem. Kids would be a lot heavier if they weren't in school," says Paul t. von Hippel, PhD, lead study author and statistician at Ohio State University. The structured school day restricts kids from the opportunity to eat and schedules regular activity time. [Explanation of the study results with the surprise included—that school helps keep kids trim.]

To prevent summer weight gain, Amy Jamieson-Petonic, RD, spokesperson for the American Dietetic Association, suggests that parents:

- Maintain the same meal schedule as during the school year. Kids are less likely to snack constantly when they follow a regular eating routine, says Jamieson-Petonic.
- Plan for daily physical activity like swimming, baseball, tag, biking, and anything that keeps kids moving.
- Limit the TV and computer time. Kids rack up more "screen time" during the summer months which may replace physical activity.
- Set specific snack times to prevent kids from grazing all day, and have a variety of low-fat, high-fiber treats available to encourage healthy choices.
- Get active as a family by swimming, biking, or hiking together.
- Sit down with your kids and develop a plan of what they would like to do over the summer, including healthy living activities, and help them stick with it. [The foregoing tips are all from Jamieson-Petonic, but note how I took the information she gave

me and made it a lot tighter to fit my word count. You can do that—take a direct quote and rewrite it in your own words—whenever you need to. Finally, a story this short doesn't always need a formal conclusion, so I omitted it, saving a few more words.]

-30-

Step 5: Turn the story in.
I turned the piece in, along with my fact-checking information. Here's what my fact-checking copy looked like:

Kelly James-Enger   278 words
[Contact info]   Rights per written contract

Does Summer Boost Snacking?

Study Finds Kids More Likely to Gain Weight Out of School

by

Kelly James-Enger

Think schools are making kids fat? Think again, according to a new study in the *American Journal of Public Health*. [See copy of study, attached.]

Researchers compared the BMI, or body mass index, of more than five thousand children at the beginning and end of kindergarten and first grade. They found that the average BMI growth per month was more than twice as fast during summer months than during the school year.

"We found that schools are part of the solution, not part of the problem. Kids would be a lot heavier if they weren't in school," says Paul t. von Hippel, PhD, lead study author and statistician at Ohio State University. The structured school day restricts kids from the opportunity to eat and schedules regular activity time. [Prior two paragraphs, Paul t. von Hippel, Ph.D., phone number 123-555-1234, paul@fakemail.com. Note: this is made-up contact info, given only to show you what I do.]

To prevent summer weight gain, Amy Jamieson-Petonic, RD, spokesperson for the American Dietetic Association, suggests that parents:

- Maintain the same meal schedule as during the school year. Kids are less likely to snack constantly when they follow a regular eating routine, says Jamieson-Petonic.
- Plan for daily physical activity like swimming, baseball, tag, biking, and anything that keeps kids moving.
- Limit the TV and computer time. Kids rack up more "screen time" during the summer months which may replace physical activity.
- Set specific snack times to prevent kids from grazing all day, and have a variety of low-fat, high-fiber treats available to encourage healthy choices.
- Get active as a family by swimming, biking, or hiking together.
- Sit down with your kids and develop a plan of what they would like to do over the summer, including healthy living activities, and help them stick with it. [All tips, Amy Jamieson-Petonic, phone number 123-555-2222; amy@fakeemail.com.]

-30-

I heard back from my editor about a week later. She was happy with the story. Yay!

Step 6: Get paid.

I received my check for $375 five weeks later.

Step 7: Get my clip.

When the story ran a few months later, I emailed both of my sources to let them know they'd been quoted, and thanked them again for their help.

The "Q & A" Article

So far we've looked at relatively simple, short pieces. The "Q & A" is another common one-source story that's relatively easy to master, as long as you get a comprehensive interview with your source. Remember you're better off having more material than you can use than not enough!

Step 1: Get the assignment.

For this story, my editor asked me to write a Q & A about the impact having a cold can have on women with incontinence or overactive bladder. The piece would run on a popular website, and I'd be paid $1/word for 450 words.

I'd written about incontinence before, so I already had an idea of what types of questions I'd include. If not, I would have conducted some background research, put together a list of possible questions, and ran them by my editor.

Let me say something about contracts here. I'd written for this health Website multiple times at this point, but its contract was horrible. It included a ridiculously broad indemnification provision (where I basically agreed to indemnify the publisher from anything and everything) that I could not get my editor to strike. "We're not allowed to change the contract," he told me.

Okay. Well, I wanted (and needed) the work, so I signed the contract and hoped that the company would never get sued over something I wrote. And to date, that hasn't happened. But I was able to change one provision of the contract—the section about rights. While the publication wanted all rights, my editor agreed that I could retain "nonexclusive reprint rights." In other words, while the website could do anything it wanted with my work, I was still able to resell those articles to other markets. [More about that in chapter 11.]

Step 2: Research the piece.

In this case, I reached out to Saint Louis University for a possible expert. I've worked with SLU's media affairs person, Nancy Solomon, for years, and she never fails to provide me with a quotable, qualified expert. Nancy arranged an interview with Mary McLennan, MD, an associate professor and director of urogynecology at Saint Louis University School of Medicine. I told Nancy in advance what the story was about so Dr. McLennan would be prepared for the interview.

As usual, I'd written out the questions I planned to base the Q & A on beforehand. Here's the transcript of our interview:

Mary McLennan, M.D., associate professor and director of the division of urogynecology at Saint Louis University School of Medicine.
[contact information omitted]
[Is there a connection between cold weather and overactive bladder? What is it?]
Cold weather tends to aggravate overactive bladder, we don't know why it is but it's kind of the mind/bladder connection the same thing you drive in the driveway, you think of the bathroom, and you have to go,
When it's cold, if someone puts her hand in the freezer or the refrigerator or the weather is cold, they feel like they have to go, we don't know why, but there's definitely a connection—kind of a mind/bladder connection
[What can people with OB do during cold weather?]
That's kind of hard—you can't move to Miami—but try to treat the overactive bladder so it's less sensitive to triggers, but there's nothing you can do for the specific condition but treating the general condition itself so it's less irritable will make less responsive to those kinds of stimuli
[What about having a cold or cough? How does that affect incontinence?]

People with stress incontinence classically leak with coughing sneezing jumping and running so if you have something aggravating those factors you're going to leak more, take a woman who may have a little leak if she sneezes, but if you have a bad cold and you're coughing all the time, you're leaking a lot more because you're increasing the pressure on the abdomen and that increases the pressure on the bladder which forces urine out

A repetitive cough is different, your pelvic floor muscles can contract fast enough to stop you from leaking, but when you cough constantly you kind of overwhelm them

[So what can people do?]

Obviously the better the pelvic floor is, the less likely you're going to leak, so doing regular floor exercises like Kegels helps, with a quick cough, the muscles will kick in but you also have to do repetitive exercises, so the muscles have the stamina to kick in multiple times, if they have bad enough incontinence or a tremendous cough, the muscles need to have more stamina to help it

Try cough suppressants to try to decrease the cough, someone who does regular pelvic floor muscles, or you may end up having surgery, for someone with incontinence who has chronic bronchitis, or chronic asthma, something that makes her cough a lot

[Anything else women can do? Or anything you want to add that you think is important?]

Takeaway message is a lot of women may not want to do something surgically but they know if they have a cold they're in a trouble, they're the one who need to do pelvic floor muscles as strong as they can be, takes 8 to 12 weeks to strengthen them , start typically 10 contractions twice a day, increase the reps by 5 a week to get to 45 twice a day, in terms of duration, most people can't hold for more than 2 seconds when they start, increase by 2 seconds, up to 6 to 8 seconds, relax in between for about five seconds

Step 3: Write the piece.

After reviewing my notes, I wrote up the 450-word Q & A, which appears below. I kept in mind what I thought readers needed to know about the connection between having a cold or cough and stress incontinence, but I forgot to address overactive bladder in the Q & A. Note that I wrote the answers to reflect what the doctor said, keeping the general meaning without worrying about perfectly exact quotes. (I ran that by my editor in advance.) Here's the finished piece:

Kelly James-Enger　　　　　　　　　　　　　　　　450 words
[contact info]　　　　　　　　　　　　　　　　　　All rights

More than a Cough: A Brief Q & A on Colds and Incontinence

by

Kelly James-Enger

If you suffer from stress incontinence, you know you can control some of the factors that can trigger a leakage problem. But what happens when you come down with a cold that leaves you coughing and sneezing—and leaking? [Brief reader-oriented lead. Or I could have used a quote from Dr. McLennan, an anecdote, or a recent statistic or study about the subject to open this piece.]

We spoke with Mary McLennan, M.D., an associate professor and director of the Division of Urogynecology at Saint Louis University School of Medicine about this common incontinence factor and how you can make it less of an issue. [This "nut graph," or "nut paragraph" tells readers what to expect from the story.]

Q: It's bad enough dealing with a cold—the stuffy head, the sneezing, the aches, and sore throat. Women with incontinence can have wetting accidents as well. What's the connection?

A: People with stress incontinence classically leak with coughing, sneezing, jumping, and running, so if you have something aggravating those factors you're going to leak more. If you have a little leak when you sneeze, with a bad cold that has you coughing all the time, you may leak a lot more. You're increasing the pressure on the abdomen [by coughing] and that increases the pressure on the bladder which forces urine out. Also, a repetitive cough is different than a single one. With one cough, your pelvic floor muscles can contract fast enough to stop you from leaking, but when you cough constantly you can kind of overwhelm them. [This first Q & A addresses the basic topic—the connection between cold weather and wetting accidents.]

Q: Other than trying to stay healthy and washing your hands frequently, what can women with stress incontinence do to lessen a cough's influence?

A: Obviously the better your pelvic floor is, the less likely you're going to leak, so doing regular pelvic floor exercises like Kegels (where you tighten the muscles that control the starting and stopping of urination) helps. You also have to do repetitive exercises so the muscles have the stamina to kick in multiple times. Taking cough suppressants to try to decrease the cough can help. And if you have stress incontinence and chronic bronchitis or chronic asthma, something that makes you cough a lot, and doing regular pelvic floor exercises doesn't help, surgery may be an option. [With this kind of story, you'll often have a "what-readers-can-do" section like this one.]

Q: How many Kegels should we do a day for the best results?

A: It takes 8 to 12 weeks to strengthen your pelvic floor muscles. You should start by doing 10 contractions twice a day, tightening your muscles for 2 seconds, relaxing for 5 between each contraction. Increase the number of contractions by 5 a week until you're doing 45 twice a day. As you get stronger, you can increase the time you tighten the muscles up to about six to eight seconds. And start off slow! If you start off gung-ho and try to do 45 a day at first, you may feel soreness or pain in that area. [Continuation of the what-readers-can-do, with specific advice.]

-30-

Step 4: Rewrite the piece.

Sometimes you'll give your editor exactly what he wants with your first attempt. In other cases, though, you'll have to do some revising. In this case, my editor felt that I spent too much time talking about Kegels, and not enough addressing overactive bladder. In retrospect, that was my mistake—I overlooked it when I was writing the piece. Oops. I apologized, and rewrote the piece that day. It was an easy rewrite as I already had the information I needed in my transcript. Here's the revised story:

Kelly James-Enger   458 words
[contact info]   Rights per written contract

REVISE:

More than a Cough: A Brief Q & A on Colds and Incontinence

by

Kelly James-Enger

If you suffer from stress incontinence, you know you can control some of the factors that can trigger a leakage problem. But what happens when you come down with a cold that leaves you coughing and sneezing—and leaking?

We spoke with Mary McLennan, M.D., an associate professor and director of the Division of Urogynecology at Saint Louis University School of Medicine about this common incontinence factor and how you can make it less of an issue.

Q: It's bad enough dealing with a cold—the stuffy head, the sneezing, the aches, and sore throat. Women with incontinence can have wetting accidents as well. What's the connection?

A: People with stress incontinence classically leak with coughing, sneezing, jumping, and running, so if you have something aggravating those factors you're going to leak more. If you have a little leak when you sneeze, with a bad cold that has you coughing all the time, you may leak a lot more. You're increasing the pressure on the abdomen [by coughing or sneezing] and that increases the pressure on the bladder which forces urine out. Also, a repetitive cough or sneeze is different than a single one. With one cough or sneeze, your pelvic floor muscles can contract fast enough to stop you from leaking, but when you cough or sneeze constantly you can kind of overwhelm them.

Q: Other than trying to stay healthy and washing your hands frequently, what can women with stress incontinence do to lessen the impact of coughing or sneezing?

A: Obviously the better your pelvic floor is, the less likely you're going to leak, so doing regular pelvic floor exercises like Kegels [where you tighten the muscles that control the starting and stopping of urination] helps. You also have to do repetitive exercises so the muscles have the stamina to kick in multiple times. Taking cough suppressants or cold medicine to ease your cough and reduce your sneezing can help. And if you have stress incontinence and chronic bronchitis or chronic asthma, conditions that make you cough a lot, doing regular pelvic floor exercises should help. If it doesn't, talk to your doctor.

Q: What about women with overactive bladder? Does having a cold or coughing and sneezing affect those women as well?

A: Actually, coughing or having a cold doesn't seem to affect women with overactive bladder—but cold *weather* can aggravate it. We don't know why, but there's definitely a connection between cold weather and urgency for some women. In fact, some will even notice that putting their hand in the freezer or refrigerator triggers an urge to urinate. Obviously you can't completely eliminate your exposure to colder temps, but treating overactive bladder will make it less sensitive to these kinds of environmental triggers.

-30-

See how I reworked the story to make my editor happy? He was pleased with this version, and I promised him I wouldn't make a similar mistake (you know, forgetting the specs of the assignment) again. I'm happy to say I continued to write for him.

Step 5: Get my clip.

The piece went online about ten days later, and I sent a copy of the URL to Dr. McLennan and to Nancy Solomon at Saint Louis University. (It's always nice to keep public relations/media affairs personnel in the loop, especially when they've helped you locate a source or other information for a story.)

Step 6: Get paid.

A few weeks after I turned in the revised edition of the story, I was paid $450. When you're writing for an online publication, which has a much shorter lead time than print publications, it's not uncommon for your story to "go live" before you're paid. The fast turnaround time makes online markets a great choice if you're new to freelancing and want to build a portfolio of clips, fast.

The Next Step

How do you feel after reading this chapter? A bit more confident that you could research and write an article? Hopefully the answer is yes. You're likely to start off with short pieces, but as you gain experience, you'll be pitching and writing longer articles. In chapters 8 and 9, we'll take a look at how to research and write them.

CHAPTER 8:
Up the Ante: Tackling Longer Articles

Last chapter, you saw how to write simple, one-source articles, so let's move on to longer, more complicated stories. Here's the thing: the process for a longer, multiple-source piece is pretty much the same as writing a short, one-piece story. The difference? You're relying on more sources and writing a longer piece. I promise, if you can write a short piece, you can write a longer one, too. (In fact, most writers find it easier to write longer articles than short ones. More words give you more flexibility.)

So let's take a look at the process:

A Feature Article

Step 1: Get the assignment.

Let's start with a piece I wrote for a trade magazine, *IGA Grocergram*. The publication is for independent grocery store owners throughout the world, so every story was written with them in mind. (Remember the first question to ask yourself before you write a piece—**who are you writing for?**)

My editor called to ask if I could write a piece on "maximizing your meat counter," and I agreed. (I didn't feel the need to mention that I was a vegetarian at the time—I figured that wasn't relevant as I could write the piece without any personal bias. If, however, you're presented with a topic that you have strong personal feelings about that may impact your work, you should turn it down—or at least inform your editor of your bias and let her decide whether she wants you to write it.)

I'd written for this market before, so I wasn't worried about the contract. The magazine paid a fair rate ($0.50/word) and purchased first N.A. serial rights, which left me free to resell the articles after they'd been published. However, because the stories were written for such a specific audience, I've never been able to resell any of them. [See chapter 12 for more about reselling your work.]

Step 2: Research the piece.

My first source was easy—my editor gave me the name and contact info of an IGA store that had initiated a "Save the Butchers" program. I visited the website to learn about the program and contacted the store owner to arrange an interview. Second, I reached out to the National Cattlemen's Beef Association, which I figured would be a good source for the story. Again, finding a source like this involves a little logic—who would be a good expert to talk about ways for grocers to sell more meat?—and some legwork. In this case, that meant contacting the National Cattlemen's Beef Association and asking to interview someone at the organization.

Before I conducted the interviews, I thought about what IGA owners would want to know and what was relevant about the topic for them. They're always concerned with improving their bottom line, staying on top of food trends, and setting themselves apart from the "big box" stores and larger supermarkets. I wrote out a short list of questions for each source, which you'll see in the transcripts below. You'll see that once again my transcript notes are rough. I don't bother with punctuation or grammar until I "pull" a quote to use it in an article.

You'll find that when you conduct an interview, some sources will give you more information than you need or easily get off-track. Other sources will be more difficult interviews and you may have to ask questions more than once, or ask them in a different way, to get usable answers. So, for example, if I had said, "tell me about your meat counter," and Bob Buonomano hadn't given me much detail, I might have followed up the question with something like, "Can you describe your meat counter to me?" or "How do your employees interact with customers who are looking for meat?"

What I want you to understand is that interviewing is a conversation between two people—you and your source—but with a purpose. As you're listening to your source, and taking notes, you're also thinking, "Is this usable? Is he answering my questions? Am I getting the information and/or quotes that I need for this piece?" Yes, you'll probably feel overwhelmed during your initial interviews. That's one reason I record all of my interviews, and then go back to fill in missing spots on my transcript later.

Here's my transcript:

Bob Buonomano, owner
Bob's Windham IGA

[Tell me about your meat counter]
Actually we're a self-service counter, we've had a combination of both over the years but the past the fifteen years it's been all self-service, I'm a firm belier in that, I think we've, I have designed several stores over the years the way I design them is our meat counters aren't in the back room, they're open to the customer, that way we can actually talk to customers while they're shopping the case and everything so we can give the service, every time a customer is in front of the case we're always saying hi to them, asking them if there's anything we can help with, things like that I think we can give them the service without having them worry about price per pound of price per packaging, etc I always tell the story, if a customer goes to the case and sees ribeyes and they need three of them and they're 9.99/pound their assumption

always is that that ribeye is going to be to be $10/steak, and if they only have $25 in their pocket, they don't want to buy three steaks, but if you weigh them out, ribeyes are only 12 ounces each, $7.50, so they can afford so if they see if in a self-service case they can make the decision without being embarrassed, so we actually try to design the store always that the meat cutter is open to the customer, helps them get the service and the perception of a personal service case but the customer can choose what they want

[I checked out the website for Save the Butchers and it looks great. How did that get started?]

Save the Butchers started a couple of years ago, we have a lot of competition in the area, we have a Wal-Mart Supermarket that was the first one in the state of CT, first superstore, we have a lot of competition but we realized that Wal-Mart wasn't cutting fresh meat in the store, meat's been my business my whole life, been cutting meat since I was fifteen years old, we always prided ourselves on quality and service and everything else and I realized that what we needed to do was to tell the customer, it wasn't good enough that I knew it, we need to tell the customer what was going on, we are what our customers think we are, no more no less, so we started this help save the butchers with the idea that , the chain stores are in a mode to get rid of cutters eventually, they want to go to centralized cutting and go to the point where they get a take a young kid in the college and teach him how to order and stock like just like it was groceries, I've trained a lot of meat cutters over the years and used to tell them as long as you're a butcher you'll always have a job, realized I might not be able to tell them that anymore, so we started the butcher's association, and did some TV advertising and newspaper ads, which worked out great, and we've got people coming in and saying I want to help save a butcher, this isn't anything we're looking to make money on or anything, what we're looking for is an identity, I think the biggest mistake retailers make is they don't tell their customers what type they are, most independent supermarkets today employ great meat cutters with a lot of experience and a lot of knowledge that I'm sure they share with their customers they just forget to highlight that in that advertising, and they don't push it, the customer needs to know what you do best, before I owned my own store, I used to run meat departments that made ¼ million dollars, I'd opened up a new store, I'd have 21 meat cutters, I'd have 3 shifts going, I'd have plenty of help, today they open a new store and they have 3 meat cutters, it's becoming a dying trade, HSTB makes the customer aware of what's going on, the Wal-Mart up the road doesn't employ a single meat cutter, the chain stores still do but nowhere near as many

Started by setting something up online, I explain to the retailers, not good enough to sell hype...step by step procedures, cleanliness and customer service, the idea of having the meat department open to the customer so you can give the perception, talking to the customers, cutting tests we've done before, inventory package, talk about gross profits, it's not just a sales ploy, the whole idea was to help the retail owners themselves who maybe didn't have the expertise to see what's going on in the meat department and get involved in it and promote the quality of it to the customer so the customer becomes involved in it, I'm convinced that the supermarkets the and chain stores have given up on meat business, they don't really want to do it if they don't have to, if there was a way to get out of the meat business and still keep the customer happy they'd do it in a second because they don't want to pay these outrageous wages with the salaries of the meat counter, I think that business is available to the independent and that that perceptions is already there with the customer, that independent stories probably have a better meat department, I'm going to my local butcher, the perception, is already there so all we're doing is just enhancing the perception

[How has Save the Butchers affected the store]

Our meat business has made us, in the past two years since we've done this, our meat department sales are up 35% and our store sales are up almost 27% [even with competition] we're growing in leaps and bounds, last month alone we were up about 20% over last year with no special promotions, no special stuff, just doing our normal sales, and doing

Help save the Butchers has done phenomenal for us if nothing else it's given us an identity, we get the best comments we get were I was told to come shop here and because you have great meat, fresh meat, it's becoming word of mouth and you need word of mouth and what we did was start the conversation

Here's the transcript from my interview with Randy Irion:

Randy Irion, Director, Retail Marketing for the National Cattlemen's Beef Association.
[contact info omitted]
[How much meat do supermarkets sell?]

There are a little over 20,000 supermarkets that do 2 million dollars a year or more in all-commodity volume, then there are another 10,000+ mom and pop stores, mostly in rural areas that are full service, they have meat counters, but they do less than 2 millions dollars a year, beyond that, you're looking at most convenience stores and most of them do not have fresh meat

Within the supermarkets, what we found that they were increasingly having both self-service and the full-service case, what we found is that the service case was in about 70& of the supermarkets, it was smaller and it was dominated by seafood, about 59% of the full service case was devoted to seafood, beef was in the next strongest position with about 17% followed by pork at 11%, chicken at 6%, and all others

[What should IGA owners keep in mind in terms of selling beef?]

For the store owner who's going to read it, beef demand is very strong, as with other protein commodities, we sell 100% of what we produce, the question is how strong-willed the demand be for it and what are people willing to pay and what we've seen is extremely strong demand in terms of very strong prices, so if I were a retailer and I was looking at my wholesale prices, I would have the confidence that consumers demand for beef in recent years has been very strong and they've demonstrated that they're willing to pay more for beef than they have historically have and I would anticipate that that would continue and I think the reasons that that is so strong is that consumers have always enjoyed the taste of beef and have recognized that with our advertising campaign our enjoyment campaign has been extremely well-received we're also now realizing that, consumers are now realizing that there's a very positive nutrition story to tell with beef, in terms of it delivering zinc, all of the B vitamins iron and protein, there are 19 cuts of beef that are actually classified as lean protein, we have a very positive nutrition story and I think that resonates with a large percentage of our audience and I think that gives them permission to go out and buy what they're always enjoyed eating in the first place so my message to the meat manager is you may be looking at historically high prices but have the high confidence that you want make sure you have available and have in stock, the major cuts of steak and hamburger and promote it because this is what customers are you looking for

I think for your store owners we recognize that people who are managing the beef counters are managing the entire counter, we did some research in 2003 that showed clearly that when the meat case labeled with nutrition information and consumers were alerted to what the various benefits were of the various protein products that they were very positively impressed, putting nutrition information on each package proved to be a positive and positively influenced meat purchase, so we are very strong supporters of making nutrition information available at the meat counter, we have a product we're very proud of.

[what else can store owners do?]

There's a program called Beef Made Easy, and available for pork products as well provides cooking information and recipes, something that the retailer makes an investment in and there are POS materials to go along with it, it's available in about 10,000 supermarkets, we developed the system with a label company... Beef Made Easy, on our retail website, beefretail.org, information available, will learn quite a bit about

I think the fact that beef demand has been up dramatically is testament to the fact that people really enjoy and recognizing it as a very, Beef is what's for Dinner and I think it's very important to looking for consumers,

Critically important, there are all kinds of consumer surveys that have been done in terms of, what causes you to choose the market that you choose, 4 things usually come to the forefront and cleanliness is right up there, with price, selection, location and cleanliness, and I don't think you can succeed without all four of those

Step 3: Research the piece

I broke my general rule of thumb for sourcing this story. Usually I use one source for stories of 300 words or fewer. For stories of 300 to 600 words, I'll typically use two sources; for stories between 600 and 1,200 words, I use three sources. Longer stories (which are becoming increasingly rare) usually require more sources, so for pieces of 1,200 to 1,800 words, I'll use four, possibly five, sources, and for longer pieces than that, as many as necessary.

For this story, however, I felt that two interviews were enough to write a solid story, especially since my editor wanted me to focus on the new "Save the Butchers" program. I could, however, had interviewed another IGA owner who had had success selling meat to offer another owner's experience. If you have any questions about how many sources you should use for a piece, ask your editor.

With my two transcripts in hand, I was ready to write. I reviewed them, making notes of strong quotes I knew I wanted to use, and organized the story by starting out with the basics of meat counters. Then I segued into the "Save the Butchers" program and offered advice for other IGA owners who want to maximize their meat sales. I chose to use subheadings (or "subheads") for the story to break it up and make it easy for readers to navigate.

Here's the piece, with some comments for you in brackets:

Kelly James-Enger 1,295 words
[contact info] Rights per written contract

Maximize your Meat Counter

by

Kelly James-Enger

In an era of super-stores and increased competition, IGA retailers need to look for every advantage over other choices shoppers have. The meat counter presents one of the biggest opportunities to build customer loyalty and increase sales, but IGA owners may not be taking advantage of their unique position to strengthen their meat counters.

Want to get more from your meat counter? Start by considering what you offer customers that your competition cannot. For example, superstores usually cut meat off-premises and don't offer hands-on service but you can position your IGA as the place to find fresh meat and helpful, experienced employees. [This two-paragraph lead is written to catch the attention of the typical IGA owner, and gives a quick overview of what the story contains.]

Self-service Versus Full-service

Many grocery stores are selling more case-ready meats that have been cut and packaged off-premises. ["Case-ready" is a term grocers will recognize—it means that the product is ready to sell and needs no further packaging. If I were writing this for a general audience, I would have defined that term.] Often there is no butcher or meat-cutter on hand to answer questions or cater to special requests. While retailers may believe this is cost-effective, the trend toward more case-ready product may hurt customer service and limit access to information that encourages customers to purchase meat.

According to Randy Irion, the director of retail marketing for the National Cattlemen's Beef Association, just over two-thirds of supermarkets have a full service case. Many have both a self-service and a full-service case, which is dominated by seafood. According to the association's research, in a typical store, 59 percent of the full service case is seafood; 17 percent is beef; 11 percent is pork; 6 percent is chicken; and 6 percent is all other meat. [These stats will be of interest to any grocer.]

If you don't offer a full service meat counter, consider the approach Bob Buonomano, owner of Bob's Windham IGA in Windham, Connecticut, has taken with his store. For the last fifteen years, Buonamono has operated a self-service meat counter—with a twist. [I identify the source with his title, which explains why readers will be interested in what he has to say.]

"I have designed several stores over the years. The way I design them, the meat counters aren't in the back room," says Buonomano. "Our meat counters are open to the customer. That way we can actually talk to customers while they're shopping the case." [Again, "shopping the case" is grocer lingo, but I needn't define it.] The butchers greet the customers, answer questions, and offer to help them with their meat needs. That gives customers the perception of a full-service counter but they're still free to choose what they want on their own.

A Novel Idea

Buonamono realized that simply having the butchers on hand wasn't enough, though. He needed to let potential customers know that his store was *the* place for excellent meat, and launched his "Help Save the Butchers" campaign to help his IGA compete against other groceries in the area. (Visit www.savethebutchers.com for info.)

His IGA has a lot of competition, but most of the stores don't cut fresh meat on the premises. Buonamono, who's been cutting meat since he was fifteen, realized that butchers may be a dying breed. "The chain stores are in a mode to get rid of cutters eventually. They want to go to centralized cutting and get to the point where...they order and stock meat like just like it was groceries," says Buonomano. "I've trained a lot of meat cutters over the years. I used to tell them, 'as long as you're a butcher you'll always have a job.' I realized I might not be able to tell them that anymore." [Note that the direct quotes I choose for the story not only give information, but do so in a lively, interesting way.]

The Help Save the Butchers Campaign has drawn new customers to his store. "It worked out great. We've got people coming in, saying, 'I want to help save a butcher!,'" he says. "What we're looking for is an identity. I think the biggest mistake retailers make is they don't tell their customers what they are. Most independent supermarkets today employ great meat cutters with a lot of experience and a lot of knowledge...store owners just forget to highlight that in their advertising." [Good tip for readers, and from someone in their shoes.]

The Right Look

An appealing meat counter is essential to draw customers. Overall, your counter should portray an image of freshness, quality, and cleanliness. That means you should cull the meat case on a daily basis and remove items that are wet, loosely or poorly wrapped, or that look unappetizing.

"There are all kinds of consumer surveys done in terms of what causes you to choose the market that you choose, and four things usually come to the forefront," says Irion. "Cleanliness is right up there with price, selection, and location. I don't think you can succeed without all four of those." [This was the last thing Irion said in our interview, and I knew when he said it that I would use it in the story. The more interviews you do, the more you'll hear quotes "pop" when you speak to someone. Your source will say something that you know you'll use for the story.]

Making the Most of your Case

While a fresh, appealing selection of meat is critical, don't overlook the design and merchandising of your meat case. For example, offering larger packages of meat may increase sales while reducing labor and supply costs—and will help build a lower price image in the minds of your customers. "No matter what size the package you put out in the case, presentation is everything," says Buonomano. "The package should always be full."

Case positioning also contributes to sales and profit. Bob suggests starting the case with pork, followed by roasts and "family pack" meats, followed by red meats and finally poultry. Putting poultry last, he explains, encourages customers to shop the entire case. "Today's customer appreciates value-added products that save preparation time or add variety to their families' meals. A well merchandised meat case must be good for both the store and the customer," says Buonomano. "Your case should offer a variety thick cut meats, thin cut meats, single pack steaks, family pack packages and sizes of roasts...merchandising is the art of finding ways to present your case and product in a way that increase sales without increasing shrink. This will put more gross dollars in the bank at the end of the week." [More tips for readers.]

Sharing Ideas and Information

Signage, nutrition information, recipes, and cooking ideas can all help customers make a decision to spend more at your meat counter. In fact, Irion says that research conducted last year found that labeling the meat case with nutrition information positively influences customer purchases. (Beef Made Easy, a Cattleman's Beef Board program, provides signage and POS information for customers; visit www.beefretail.org for more information.)

In addition to nutrition information and serving ideas, make sure you're using appropriate signage. "Signage should not only be reserved for sales items," says Buonamono. In addition to sale items, hamburger, and family packaged meats, high-volume items with everyday low prices should have signage to draw customers' attention." [More tips.]

Create your Meat Niche

Buonomano believes that many supermarkets and chain stores have "given up" on the meat business. "They don't really want to do it if they don't have to...I think that business is available to the independent," he says. "That perception is already there with the customer—that independent stores probably have a better meat department. All we're doing is enhancing the perception."

He adds that a program like Help Save the Butchers can help IGA owners get more from their advertising dollars. "Advertising is a very expensive portion of our business today. So when you do advertise, you want your customer to recognize your ads as quick as possible," says Buonomano. "The idea behind Help Save the Butchers is that when your customer wants quality meats for their family's everyday meals or a special cut that only a butcher can help with, they will know that your store is the place to shop." [Great quotes and great idea for readers.]

Since its inception, the program has produced phenomenal results, says Buonamono. "In the past two years since we've done this, our meat department sales are up 35% and our store sales are up almost 27%," he says. "Last month alone we were up about 20% over last year with no special promotions, just doing our normal sales...if nothing else, Help Save the Butchers has given us an identity.

"We get the best comments like, 'I was told to come shop here because you have great, fresh meat,'" he adds. "It's becoming word of mouth and you need word of mouth. What we did was start the conversation." [Simple quote to close the story.]

-30-

Step 4: Turn in the story.
After writing the piece, I turned it in to my editor. She was happy with the overall structure and ran the piece with just a few minor edits. She didn't require me to turn in fact-checking material, but I had it on hand just in case.

Step 5: Get paid.
I was paid $600 a few weeks later.

Step 6 Get my clip.
When the story was published, I made a copy and sent it to Randy Irion, thanking him for his time. Although I knew that Bob Buonomano would see the piece in *IGA Grocergram*, I sent him an email reminding him about it. I always notify sources when a story runs; to me, that's basic manners. It also helps them remember me if I ever need to interview them again in the future.

Remember the process of writing an article for a trade publication isn't any different than writing for a consumer or custom magazine. The only difference is that you're writing for a specialized, niche audience who assume that you know their business. If you have a background in a particular profession or industry, I suggest you consider writing for trades. The pay may not be as high as for consumer markets, but I've found that once you get in with a publication, it's easier to get steady work and the stories are relatively easy to report and write.

Another Feature
In the nearly 16 years I've been freelancing, I've seen articles get shorter and shorter. I used to write features of 1,800 to 2,000 words, even 2,500 words, on a regular basis. Now for most markets, a full-length feature clocks in at about 1,300 words (even fewer than that for online markets).

So let's discuss a feature that would be relatively easy for even a new writer to tackle, and break it down step by step.

Step 1: Pitch the idea.
Since I became a parent seven years ago, I occasionally pitch and write parenting stories. Almost every idea comes from my own experience as a parent, but that's not enough to support an article. (If I were writing an essay, then

my personal experience would probably be sufficient. For an article, though, usually your personal experience is only the starting point.)

I've always been afraid of heights, so taking a climbing class with my then four-year-old son was a big deal for me. I found I loved climbing, which made me realize I'd held back from trying other activities at the gym out of fear—usually fear of looking stupid. Then I thought, hey, that could be a great idea for a parenting story—a story about how pushing yourself to take risks can actually benefit you.

I pitched the idea, with a brief lead, to one of my regular editors at a regional parenting magazine.

Step 2: Get the assignment.

My editor loved the idea, and assigned the piece for $350 at 1,300 words. This may seem like a low rate compared to some of my other markets. But the stories don't take me much time to research and write, so it's worth it to me. While freelancers are usually paid per-word, I focus on what I make per-hour, not per-word. If I can write a story that pays $350 in three to four hours, I'm making $75 to $100/hour, an excellent hourly rate. On the other hand, some assignments that pay more *per-word* wind up paying less *per-hour*. Don't worry about your hourly rate starting out, but as you gain experience, you'll want to start paying attention to which assignments pay a higher hourly rate.

Step 3: Research the assignment.

I've done a fair amount of writing about psychology topics like this, so I went back through some older stories to see if I had interviewed any strong experts for other stories in the past. That's how I came up with the two psychologists I used for this story. Otherwise, I would have used the techniques I shared in the "One-source article" example in chapter 7. I interviewed both psychologists about risk-taking, the benefits and drawbacks of taking risks, and the advice about risk-taking they'd give to parents reading the article.

However, I also needed at least one real person anecdote, and those are often harder to locate. In this case, I put out an email blast to a bunch of local moms to see if any of them could talk about their personal experience taking a risk—or knew someone who might be willing to talk to me. I quickly found a mom who fit the bill, and interviewed her a couple of days later.

If I'd been writing for a national magazine, though, I would have had to cast a wider net. Once again you can use a source like HARO [see chapter 7] to request an anecdotal source, but I've had better success using Facebook or simply sending an email to some of my friends throughout the country. I'd say something like, "Hey, gang—I'm doing a story for a fitness magazine on how kettle bells can help you lose weight. Do you know a woman in her 20s or 30s who has lost weight doing a kettle bell workout who would be willing to talk to me? Let me know in the next couple of days, and thanks so much!" I've used this method to find dozens of anecdotal sources over the years, and have helped other writers locate sources when they request my help as well.

Step 4: Write the article.

I'd already envisioned the format of the article by the time I sat down with my transcripts to write the piece. I would:

- Open with a first-person lead about climbing with Ryan;
- Include a nut graph that explained that risk-taking was often beneficial;
- Discuss the advantages of risk-taking;
- Discuss any negative aspects of risk-taking;
- Describe how to analyze the risk of a certain action; and
- Give advice about risk-taking specifically for parents.

Writing the piece took me less than two hours, and I used subheadings to break the piece up and help orient readers. Here it is:

Kelly James-Enger 1,330 words
[contact info] Rights per contract

Embrace your Inner Thrill Seeker:

How Taking Risks Can be Good for You

by

Kelly James-Enger

I admit it—I'm more than a little afraid of heights. But last year, I found out that my local Y was offering a parent/child climbing class—and my son, then four, had been wanting to try the climbing wall. After watching Ryan effortlessly scramble up, I triple-checked my safety harness, wiped my sweaty hands on my shorts, and started my first climb.

I could feel my heart pounding in my ears, and forced myself not to look down as I climbed higher, slowly searching for my next handhold. I was shocked—and exhilarated—to discover that I'd made it to the top of the 25-foot wall on my first try!

I decided then to stretch myself more—in short, to take more risks (though I have no intention of going sky-diving any time soon.) Since then, I've started taking Spinning and yoga classes, two activities I'd always been nervous about trying. [The first three paragraphs are the first-person lead.]

When psychologists study risk-taking behavior, it's often in the context of things like taking drugs, engaging in unprotected sex, driving too fast, and other activities that can have fatal consequences. So it's not surprising that we tend to think of risk-taking as overly dangerous. However, reasonable risk-taking can help you break out of a rut and lead to greater confidence as a woman—and help you be an excellent role model for your children. [Here's the nut graph, which sums up what readers can expect from the story.]

The Rewards of Risk

You don't have to scale a wall or speak in front of 300 people to feel like you're taking a risk. "Risk-taking is a way of going out of your comfort zone," says clinical psychologist Monica Ramirez Basco, Ph.D., author of *The Procrastinator's Guide to Getting Things Done* (2010, Gilford). "We limit ourselves by our perceptions of ourselves. If we perceive ourselves as being good at certain things we want to do them—and if we perceive that we're not as good at other things, we tend to shy away from them." [Great quote which introduces why risk is scary.]

It makes sense, right? No one likes to look stupid, and the bigger the risk, the scarier it can seem. Your personal risk-taking quotient depends on your personality, the size and type of risk, and how you grew up. "If you're in a home environment where people are encouraged to try new things…in that kind of arena, more risk-taking is possible," says Basco. "But if the risk is too great or the risk of criticism is too high, you may not be willing to do it." [Explanation of why some of us take more risks than others.]

The potential rewards of a risk will also determine whether you're willing to take it. When Julie Devine moved to Downers Grove, she didn't know anyone in the area. She'd been a working mom until her second daughter was born and she decided to stay home with her children. "We had moved here when I was pregnant with Jillian, and I just never met anyone because I worked," says Devine, 36. "So after Lainey was born, and I was home with two, and suddenly feeling more and more isolated, I started stalking the neighborhood on daily walks, trying to spy who had similar toddler toys in their yards. After a few weeks of daily walks, I made up fliers and put them in the mailboxes of the homes I'd identified – total strangers to me – inviting them to my house for a playgroup."

Devine says it felt like a risk to reach out to people she didn't know, but her effort was rewarded. "All six moms showed up, and four of them ended up being some of my best friends," she says. "We're still friends five and a half years later, and so are all the kids!" [This is a great anecdote. First, she's a fellow mom who did something scary. Second, that risk turned out great for her. See how her real-life experience supports the story?]

Risk as Part of Life

You may not think of yourself as a risk-taker, like the firefighters, police officers, pilots, and soldiers who encounter danger almost every day. Yet, "risk-taking behavior is what moves the world forward. No change happens if someone doesn't take a risk," says psychotherapist Tina B. Tessina, PhD, (aka "Dr. Romance"), author of *Money, Sex and Kids: Stop Fighting about the Three Things That Can Ruin Your Marriage* (Adams Media, 2008). In fact, even loving someone is a risk, because you might get hurt, she points out. And is there any bigger emotional risk than becoming a parent? [I wanted readers to recognize that we all take risks, even if we would rather avoid them.]

"Any time we learn something new, we are taking a risk—moving outside the comfort zone," says Tessina. "Learning new things keeps us motivated, alive, energized. We need a certain (perhaps small) amount of risk to be happy."

As a parent, there's another issue as well—you want your children to understand how to evaluate risks so they know the difference between healthy and unhealthy risk-taking. It starts with teaching your children not to touch a stove, or to look both ways and hold a grownup's hand before crossing the street. But as your children get older, they need to be able to make decisions (like wearing their seat belts, saying "no" to drugs and alcohol, and staying safe online) to stay safe and healthy. Even if you hate taking risks, you must expect your children to want to experiment with "scary" behaviors—that's a normal part of adolescence. [This is aimed directly at my readers—parents of young kids.]

Look (and Plan) Before You Leap

If taking risks scare you, start off gradually. "In fact, it's better to take risks in increments," says Basco. "If you're worried about failure don't take a giant leap—just take a small step. Sometimes it's just gathering information."

That information helps you determine the risk/benefit ratio. What are the potential benefits of taking the risk? Could the experience be fun, help you grow, or make your life more interesting? And consider the potential risks. Could you lose money, invest your time in something that turns out to be worthwhile, or look foolish (at least in your own eyes?) Consider Julie Devine—she could have worried about looking needy or lonely to her neighbors. Instead, she wound up with lifelong friends. [Now we get into how to analyze and take risks.]

Show your kids how you evaluate risks. For example, if you're training for a 5k race for the first time, you might say that you're nervous about not being able to finish, but that you're excited about challenging yourself in a new way. "Learn to take calculated risks yourself, so you can teach your kids from what you know from your own experience," says Tessina. "Talk to your kids about the benefits and problems associated with risk. Compare the reckless risks of drugs and extreme behavior with the risks that bring rewards, like trying something new, loving someone, or being emotionally open." [Advice geared specifically for parents.]

And if you're not a risk-taker by nature, don't worry—you don't have to suddenly ditch your usual routine in favor of a new job, a new home, and a new hairstyle all at once. "Make it a calculated risk—figure out in advance what you might lose or gain," says Tessina. "Take small risks at first, if you're not used to it, and grow into the bigger risks."

Those bigger risks—the ones that take you outside of your comfort zone—can feel scary at first. But they'll also help you grow as a person, and help teach your kids to embrace appropriate risks—while hopefully avoiding the ones that can be truly dangerous. [The close reminds readers that appropriate risk-taking isn't just good for them; modeling it will help their children as well.]

-30-

Step 5: Turn the piece in.
I turned in the story, along with my backup material. My editor was happy with the piece, which wasn't surprising—I've written for her for years and I know what she wants. During all that time, I've only had to revise one story, which is another reason I'm willing to take a relatively low per-word rate for these stories. My per-hour rate remains relatively high.

Step 6: Get my clip.
The story ran several months later.

Step 7: Get paid.
I was paid $350 within a week of its publication. As always, I notified and thanked my sources.

Another Longer Feature

I'd like to share one other longer story in this chapter, a health-related feature. While this story requires a little more research, it's not that complicated, and I think even a new writer could tackle this type of piece once you've sold and written some shorter ones.

Step 1: Get the assignment.
I'd been writing fitness and nutrition articles for a fitness magazine for several years when my editor there asked me to cover the topic of childhood obesity. She wanted a story of 1,600 words for $0.75/word.

I agreed, and spoke with her briefly about what she wanted from the piece. While I pitch about half of the assignments I wind up writing, the other half start out as my editors' ideas. That's fine with me, but I'm always sure to confirm what my editor wants before I start working on a piece. Some editors will send a detailed assignment letter; others just tell you in a few lines what they want. Either way, make sure you're on the same page as far as the topic, angle, and structure for the story go.

Step 2: Research the story.

I started by looking at government health sites like the Centers for Disease Control and Prevention (www.cdc.gov). There I found statistics and background information about childhood obesity at http://www.cdc.gov/obesity/childhood/index.html. Then I used Profnet to identify and contact several physicians who specialize in treating overweight and obese kids, and called the American Dietetic Association for a referral to a spokesperson.

Step 3: Interview my sources.

I conducted the interviews with my three sources, focusing on the causes of pediatric obesity and how parents could combat it. Each interview took about fifteen minutes to complete. As usual, I sent thank-you notes afterwards.

Step 4: Write the piece.

My initial background research had given me a better understanding of why kids today are fat, and getting fatter. Reading through my transcripts and other research, I thought about how to organize the story. Initially I decided to use a brief lead, describe the growing problem of childhood obesity, the risks of being overweight or obese as a kid, and then discuss what parents could do about the problem. That seemed the most logical way to write the piece. I used subheads to break up the story, as you'll see below:

Kelly James-Enger   1,710 words (w/sidebar)
[Contact info]   First N.A. rights

Chubby Children:

Why Today's Kids are Getting Fatter

and What Parents Can do

by

Kelly James-Enger

Today's kids are fatter than they've ever been before. According to recent statistics, 20.6 percent of preschoolers, 30.3 percent of children ages 6-11, and 30.4 percent of adolescents ages 12-17 are overweight—and a report of the Surgeon General found that nearly half of all teenagers aren't vigorously active on a regular basis. Add cutbacks in physical education programs and countless hours spent watching television, and you've got millions of overweight kids—and that number continues to grow. [This is what I call a "startling statistic" lead that will hopefully grab the reader's attention, even if she's not a parent.]

Some parents may dismiss these concerns as simply "baby fat" that their children will outgrow. But overweight kids are also at higher risk for a variety of medical problems that may continue on into adulthood. What's causing this problem? And what can parents and other concerned adults do to help keep their children fit and healthy? [The nut graph, which sets out the story to come.]

The Roots of the Problem

There are a number of causes of the rise in pediatric obesity in this country, says pediatric endocrinologist Frank Diamond, MD, of the University of South Florida College of Medicine in Tampa, Florida. "We know that there is a genetic predisposition to excessive weight gain and we're learning every day about new biochemistry that controls the way the body manages its weight maintenance, but the population changes have occurred over a period of about 25 years, and genes don't change that fast," says Dr. Diamond. "What appears to be happening is changes in lifestyle superimposed on a population with genetic susceptibility."

Those changes in lifestyle include children exercising less while they spend more time engaged in sedentary activities, and an increase in both overall caloric intake and high-fat, high-carbohydrate foods. This adds up to a startling percentage of overweight kids. "Pediatric obesity is a problem. Anywhere from 25 to 35 percent of children, depending on the ethnic group you look at are overweight, and somewhere between 10 to 12 percent are obese," says Dr. Diamond. "There are a substantial number of children for whom increased body fat is a health problem." [The preceding two paragraphs introduce why kids are getting fatter, and we hear from a qualified expert on the subject.]

There are a number of factors causing kids to eat more and use fewer calories, says registered dietitian Sheah Rarback of Miami, a spokesperson for the American Dietetic Association. "Portion sizes have grown tremendously over the past few decades. Restaurants and drive-throughs serve huge portions," says Rarback. And as more parents rely on eating out to feed their families, children consume more restaurant food. That translates into more calories, and more high-fat meals.

Even at schools, children have access to vending machines that offer soda, candy, and chips. Kids who are alone after school may turn to these same kinds of foods as snacks. "The foods are there without any parental guidance of what to eat and how much to eat, so this also makes for extra calories," says Rarback. [More dietary reasons for chubby children, with another expert weighing in.]

Complicating matters is that today's kids aren't as active as children used to be, either. "In addition to being given all of these opportunities to eat more, there are fewer opportunities to use calories," says Rarback. Physical education classes are no longer a requirement for most schools, and budget constraints have forced many elementary programs to cut back on gym time. Children who live in dangerous neighborhoods may be encouraged to stay inside, and most kids no longer walk to school—they're driven or take the bus.

And don't forget the television. The more television a child watches, the more likely he is to be overweight. The popularity of computer and video games also encourage sedentary activities over more active ones. "What has become a major source of entertainment for children are video games and computer games and they are very sedentary," says Rarback. "Fifteen years ago kids might have gone over and played ball in the street and now they play Playstation. All the computers, and the Playstations and X-boxes are all sitting-down activities. We've been hit on both fronts." [The next two paragraphs look at the other side of the equation—that in addition to eating more calories and eating more high-fat foods, kids aren't as active as before.]

Research shows that low birth-weight babies have a higher chance of becoming overweight kids, and heredity may also play a role. If you have an obese parent, you're more likely to be obese as a child. Researchers believe there may also be a combination of gene defects that may make people susceptible to obesity, but they haven't yet determined what that combination of genes may be. [I'm not quoting an expert here, but all of this information came from my background research and interviews. Remember as a freelancer you don't have to attribute everything in an article. The reader assumes you've done the research and are an expert of sorts.]

The Health Risks Multiply

Simply put, fat kids are more likely to have certain health problems than normal weight kids. One of the biggest risks is type II diabetes, where your body doesn't make enough insulin or can't use it properly. "We're in the midst of a very dramatic increase in type II diabetes in children and that's been attributed to the increasing body weight in children," says Dr. Diamond. "Clearly increased body fat makes you more resistant to insulin and puts you at greater risk for type II diabetes, particularly if you've got an underlying genetic susceptibility."

Being overweight also increases blood pressure, which increases the risk of cardiovascular disease. There are orthopedic risks as well—overweight kids are more likely to have problems with their hips and orthopedic disorders like bowing of the tibia and femur bones. These children can also develop sleep apnea, which causes changes in their breathing pattern in the night and they don't sleep well, which makes them more tired during the day.

Many girls who become overweight develop polycystic ovary syndrome, which is a condition where the ovaries produce too much of the male hormone testosterone. Obese children also have higher levels of cholesterol and more than half of them have at least one risk factor for cardiovascular disease. In addition to the health risks, many overweight kids face teasing from their classmates and suffer from poor self-esteem or body image.

Finally, if you're an overweight kid, you're also more likely to be an overweight adult. "We certainly know that it tends to track into adulthood, the older and heavier you are, the more likely you are to become an obese adult," says Dr. Diamond. "So an obese six-year-old has a certain risk of becoming an obese adult, and that risk is much higher if you're an obese twelve-year-old. If you've already got high blood pressure or upper limit blood pressure when you're 12, you're more likely to have hypertension as an adult, and most cardiovascular disease probably does start in childhood." [This section describes the health risks for fat kids, with a mix of direct quotes and exposition. You'll see this technique is nearly every nonfiction article.]

What Parents Can Do

While the odds may be stacked against kids, there are ways to help your children stay fit—or lose weight if they need to. "Because there are a number of causes or reasons for kids to be overweight, there's not one quick fix," says Rarback. "We need multiple solutions or a comprehensive solution because multiple issues have put us in this sorry state we're in right now." [Intro into this section.]

First, parents should avoid presuming that the problem is solely their child's. "Parents have to say that this is an issue that's affecting the health of our *family*," says Rarback. "They shouldn't point the finger at the child and say 'you're overweight and *you* have a problem.' It's a family thing." If you want your child to eat healthier, you must have healthier choices available, so clear your home of high-fat, high-calorie junk foods, and offer more nutritious options instead.

"When kids come home from school, they're hungry and they're going to snack on the first thing they see," says Rarback. Have pre-bagged snacks for your children to eat like baby carrots with dip or a mini-yogurt with cereal. Also, make it a habit to eat dinner together as a family so your children can start modeling appropriate eating behavior. That means teaching kids appropriate portion sizes, and encouraging them to eat more vegetables and fruits while cutting back on empty calories. [Here, parents get practical advice—it's the "how-to" part of this story.]

Also, make sure that you don't use food as a reward or punishment—or as a distraction. "Food shouldn't be used to change the mood, cheer a child up, or keep him quiet," says Rarback. "Think of the message you're sending."

Helping your child become more active takes more than saying, "go outside and play." "Become an active family," says Rarback. "Even if parents don't have weight issues, exercise is good for you, no matter what you weigh. Model an active lifestyle." That may mean taking a walk after dinner, playing catch with your kids, or going bike-riding on Saturday mornings. Look for ways to make your regular family occasions more physical.

Limiting the amount of sedentary activities like television watching and playing on the computer also helps. "There's a direct correlation between number of hours the child watches TV every day and their percentage of body fat," says Dr. Diamond. "Encourage children to get outside after school and exercise. Ask your schools to put phys ed back in the curriculum. [More suggestions for parents.]

Preventing weight problems before they begin reduces your child's risk of becoming overweight. Parents should weigh their kids regularly, and talk to their pediatrician about what a healthy weight for their children is. Children at the 85th percentile or higher of average weight for their age are considered overweight; children at the 95th percentile or higher are considered obese. [Good advice for parents, but in retrospect, I could have included the description of overweight and obese kids earlier in the story. That would have been more logical.]

The bottom line to combat this growing problem is that parents need to set a healthy example for their children to learn from. "A number of studies confirm that when the parents become involved in activity with their children and follow the same meal plan as the children, weight control is much more successful," says Dr. Diamond. "The parents can't expect the kids to limit what they eat if the parents themselves are sitting on the couch with a big bag of chips. You have to set an example for your kids." [Simple but strong close.]

SIDEBAR: What Parents Can Do [Set every sidebar off with a separate header]

Want to encourage your kids to eat healthier and be more active? Try these simple tips:

- Limit fast food meals. The large portions and high-fat meals pack on pounds.
- Don't use food as a reward. If you want to treat your child, suggest a shared activity together instead.
- Have plenty of healthy snacks at home. Kids are more likely to eat nutritious foods when they're easily available.
- Set a good example. Demonstrate healthy eating and exercise habits for your kids.
- Teach kids about the difference between hunger and appetite. Have them check to see if they're physically hungry before they eat something. [I decided to include a sidebar of what parents could do to accompany the story, but I could have also written a sidebar that included online resources for parents or some simple, healthy, kid-friendly recipes.]

-30-

Step 5: Turn the story in.
I turned in the story to my editor. After she told me she was happy with it, I sent along my fact-checking information.

Kelly James-Enger

Step 6: Get paid.
I was paid $1,200 three weeks later.
Step 7: Get my clip.
This story ran five months later, and I notified my sources about it.
Step 8: Get paid—again.

With this story, there's an additional step. Because I sold first N.A. serial rights to the piece, I was free to resell it to other markets once it was originally published. And I have, five times since then. Each time, I updated the statistics in the lead, but otherwise the story is an "evergreen," or a story that doesn't go out of date very quickly. Compare that to a story like the piece on NEAT I shared in chapter 7; because it's based on a new study, it's going to be outdated quickly.

The Reslanting Process

When I talked about queries in chapter 3, I mentioned that one of the easiest ways to work more efficiently is to write more than one story about the same basic idea. Maybe you've already reslanted your idea by pitching more than one noncompeting market with different spins on your topic. If not, take the initial idea and think about other ways to approach it, and then consider what markets might be interested in it. Or you can try the process in reverse, and think about markets you're familiar with and how to reslant the idea to interest them.

Believe me, no matter how narrow an idea may seem, there is always another angle to take with it. For example, let's talk about the topic of gratitude. I was reading a health-related blog and came across a brief mention of a study that examined the connection between gratitude and health. It appeared that expressing gratitude appeared to produce emotional and physical health benefits.

As a longtime believer in thank-you notes, this study caught my attention, and it was just the kind of psychology topic I like to read—and write—about. I hadn't done any additional research at this point, so my story idea was that little nugget—"being grateful makes you healthy."

So what kind of readers would be interested in this topic? As a mom who's teaching her kids about the importance of manners, I immediately thought of parenting markets. Health magazines, and general interest publications that cover health (and there are a lot of them) were also possibilities. Maybe there was a spiritual dimension to the topic I could explore for a religious-themed publication, or I could pitch a food magazine with a Thanksgiving-themed angle.

Get the idea? You start with the nugget of an idea, and go from there. Regardless of whether you choose an angle and then find a market, or do the process in reverse, always look for more than one way to spin a story idea. You may be surprised at how many ways you can approach one idea. Take caffeine. In the span of several months, I wrote about caffeine's health benefits for a custom magazine; about caffeine addiction for a major newspaper; about how caffeine was popping up in beauty products for a consumer publication; and about how caffeine can help improve athletic performance for a sports magazine.

Each story required some research and interviews, but the more I wrote about caffeine, the more I learned, and the easier it was for me to come up with new spins on the subject. You'll find the same is true as you delve deeper into any subject. The more you know about it, the more ideas spring forth.

You'll almost always end up with material that never makes it into your first piece. You may only cull two or three quotes from an interview transcript, and you'll have background research that you can reuse for other articles.

So let's look at one example of how I wrote two stories about the same basic idea for two different markets:

Step 1: Pitch the idea.

I went on PubMed to get a copy of the abstract of the article I'd seen referenced online. While there, I did a quick search on "gratitude and health," and found several other relevant study abstracts I printed out for future reference. I pitched the idea to several markets, including *The Chicago Tribune*. That query appears below:

Dear Ms. Joyce:

I've been using sign language with my son since he was about six months old. Today, at nearly two, he knows about thirty signs including "please" (rubbing his open hand in a circle on his chest), "doggy" (wagging his index finger like a tail), "flower" (finger and thumb briefly touch back and forth under his nose), and "car" (positioning his hands like he's holding a steering wheel). Lately we've been working on "thank you," which he knows but has to be reminded to use. [This first-person lead fits with the angle I'm taking—a piece aimed at parents.]

In fact, children aren't born with an innate desire to express thanks—as parents, we teach it to them. But it turns out that gratitude may be more than just good manners. New research shows that it can provide both emotional as well as physical health benefits. For example, in one study, college-aged participants who regularly listed five things they were grateful for felt better about their lives and had fewer physical complaints than people who simply listed five neutral events. [This paragraph explains why readers will be interested in the article idea.]

"Get Grateful: How it Helps your Health" will report on this fascinating area of research, and give practical ways to implement gratitude in readers' daily lives. I plan to interview gratitude experts such as Gitendra Uswatte, Ph.D., assistant professor of psychology at the University of Alabama at Birmingham, for this story; although I estimate 800 words for this story, that's flexible depending on your needs. A possible sidebar might include easy ways for families to practice gratitude. [This "nuts and bolts" section describes how I plan to approach the story.]

Interested in this story for the "Health" section of Q? I'm a fulltime freelancer in the Chicago area; my health, fitness, and nutrition stories have appeared in magazines including *Redbook, Self, Health, Continental, Fitness, Woman's Day,* and *Shape,* and I'll be happy to send clips upon request. I hope you'll agree this is a great topic for an upcoming section of Q. [My ISG demonstrates that I've read the newspaper, and highlights some of my recent experience.]

Please let me know if you have any questions about the idea; otherwise, I'll be in touch shortly with a few other story ideas.

All best,
Kelly James-Enger

Step 2: Get the assignment.

Great news! Not only did I get the assignment from *The Chicago Trib* (600 words at $0.50/word), I also had a custom magazine ask me to write a longer piece on the health benefits of gratitude (1,200 words at $1.50/word). With two assignments in hand, I was ready to research and write both pieces.

Step 3: Research both pieces.

I contacted Dr. Uswatte and Dr. Robert Emmons, another researcher who had been studying gratitude and health, and arranged to interview both of them. In Emmons' case, he asked that I send him questions via email instead of a phone interview, which I agreed to.

Their brief transcripts appear below.

Gitendra Uswatte, Ph.D.
[contact info omitted]
[how do you define gratitude?]
Emotion that reflects thankfulness for benefits received from other individuals or could be nature or a higher being

We don't think of it as simply as saying thank you or being appreciative that way that's certainly one level, in this study we worked with vets with post-traumatic who had had PTSD for many years, Vietnam, severe chronic disabilities or mental disorders so one might expect that positive psychology these positive aspects of wellbeing wouldn't be so important for this population dealing with this group of people with a severe mental disorder, You might think this is important for healthy folks but not so much for people with a severe mental disorder what we found was that vets with PTSD on average had lower levels of gratitude than vets without PTSD, having gratitude was still important for their well-being, so those vets who reported experiencing gratitude more frequently also reported a greater satisfaction with life, engaged in a greater level of rewarding social activity, and other activities that were rewarding in themselves, so we found that gratitude even in this population was strongly related to well-being

Q [Are you aware of other research in this area or is there anyone else I should talk to?]

Research done by Mark Seligman and colleagues showing that that really a rather simple exercise can make a big difference in well-being and it's called the 3 blessings experience, involves at the end of each day writing down three good things that happened and why they happened, what the source of the benefit what was the reason of those good things happening, simple exercise but found that when done daily has powerful and long-lasting effects on people's level of happiness and deceasing levels of depression, level of happiness, satisfaction, published in American Psychologist 2005

Q [are you conducting/planning other research?]

A We're thinking about is developing interventions to increase gratitude and I'm interested in looking at patients and caregivers and how gratitude benefits both

Q [do you think it's important for children to learn gratitude?]

A I think it's a strength that's important for families because we tend to take each other for granted in families, so I think it's something especially helpful to help members of families, parents and children, not take each for granted, I think it does help to take a different perspective on the riches that are available to us

Q [give me examples of what parents can do to teach gratitude]

A I think there are some simple things parents can do, simply asking your child what are the good things that happened today, tell me about the good things that happened today, something as simple as that, making that a daily habit to ask, helps the child focus their attention, I think there's an exercise that has shown to be effective in randomized controlled experiment, and that is called the 3 blessings exercise, that's something children can do as well as adults, I think for parents when thinking about whether this is something important to teach their children is to consider the research showing that this is a strength that is strongly linked to life satisfaction so adults who are high in gratitude tend to be highly satisfied with their lives, and so for most parents, their strongest wish is for their child to be happy and this is a quality that's been strongly linked to happiness

To: Robert Emmons, PhD [via email]
Q [contact info omitted]
[First off, how do *you* define gratitude?]

A I've found it very helpful to conceive of it in terms of two stages. First, gratitude is the *acknowledgment* of goodness in one's life. In gratitude we say yes to life. We affirm that all things taken together, life is good and has elements that make it worth living. Second, gratitude is *recognizing* that the source(s) of this goodness lie at least partially outside the self. The object of gratitude is other-directed; one can be grateful to other people, to God, to animals, but never to oneself.

[Based on your research, what are some of the emotional health benefits of gratitude?]

Our research has shown that grateful people experience higher levels of positive emotions such as joy, enthusiasm, love, happiness and optimism and, that the practice of gratitude as a discipline protects a person from the destructive impulses of envy, resentment, greed, and bitterness. We have discovered that a person who experiences gratitude is able to cope more effectively with everyday stress, may show increased resilience in the face of trauma-induced stress, and may recover more quickly from illness and benefit from greater physical health.

[But there are physical health benefits, as well? Correct? What are they?]

When people are grateful, they experience "calm energy"--they feel more alert, alive, interested, enthusiastic. They feel more alive and vital. People often report feeling grateful for their bodies--for the ability to see, smell, hear, and so on. Some of these effects can be quantified: They sleep 1/2 hour more per evening, awake feeling more refreshed, and in a remarkable finding they exercise 33% more each week compared to persons who are not keeping these journals.

[And what would your advice be for ways to people to become more grateful/incorporate more gratitude into their daily lives?]

Despite all the benefits, it can be difficult to practice gratitude on a daily basis. Some days it comes naturally; other days, it feels like we're taking our medicine, doing something that's good for us but that we don't really like. Practice keeping a gratitude journal until it becomes a natural habit. This might be difficult at first (like any type of exercise) but then you find that focusing on gratitude leads to having more to be grateful about. Psychological research has shown that translating thoughts into concrete language (i.e. words, whether oral or written) has advantages over just thinking the thoughts. Making a "what-I-take-for-granted" list can also be helpful. It really comes down to a choice, but it also takes dedicated practice to reframe one's thinking in this way, since we seem programmed to think in terms of dissatisfaction, deprivation, and discontent.

I had the "expert" interviews completed, and felt that I had what I needed for the story for the custom magazine. However, I still needed a "real person" anecdote for the *Tribune* story—a parent who thought it was important to teach gratitude to his or her children. I reached out to friends and neighbors and got the name of a local mom who agreed to talk to me.

Here's that transcript, with some identifying information omitted:

Heather Isacson
4 children, Noah 10 in Aug, Clay 8.5, Reese 5 In Sep Annika, 2 in Sep
[how do you define gratitude?]

To me and in our family is to be thankful for what we have, and to make our children understand the difference between needs and wants and not to take advantage or forget about things that we have or other people don't have, the little things that we take for granted we try to focus on, how lucky they are that we have, bicycles, and that we're healthy, having examples of people of who are less fortunate but to actually see it, that's a big difference, thank you and you're welcome, thank you and God bless you, are all in our everyday vocabulary,

[Do your kids send thank-you notes?]

absolutely and thank you notes are for more than just gifts, Noah wrote a thank you note to his coach, they both write thank-you note to their coaches, we point out that those people volunteer a lot of time, and they don't need to do that but they do it, and they do it because, to know that they're appreciated, I don't even have to ask, Noah said he wanted to,

[tell me about your kids' parties. Do you donate the gifts?] We don't have gifts, that started with Noah, when he turned five, he wanted to have a birthday party, you can have a party and invite all of these children, however we're going to ask that they bring that these kids not bring birthday gifts and he said that's fine, I don't need gifts, so I said what would you like people to bring, maybe they could bring school supplies, we've had his party guests bring school supplies, Sharing Connections, and sharing connections, and local schools, hand-deliver it, the other thing that we've been involved with basketball tournament, all four of them American Cancer Society, were exposed to volunteering and doing things, they were there and helping, so volunteering and charity is a party of our family life, Clay, his birthday is in January, mittens and hats and gloves, Reese, exposed to that at the first time, that will be his intention to help

I think my children appreciate the sun shining more so than the average child, they appreciate a beautiful day, look how beautiful that is, and I don't know many five year olds like that

Step 4: Write both pieces.

I wrote the story for the custom magazine first. Because I sold all rights to it, I cannot include it in this book, but I can tell you that I organized the story by writing a brief lead that included the line, "researchers are finding that experiencing gratitude provides a host of emotional and even physical health benefits." Then I wrote several paragraphs describing how researchers define gratitude, and gave an overview of the studies that showed a link between expressing gratitude and improved mood and health. Finally, I included a section that readers could use to become more grateful in their day-to-day lives.

For the second story, I decided to use a first-person lead, similar to the one in my query letter. This was my choice but I could have chosen to use Heather Isacson as a third-person lead, or started by mentioning one of the recent studies. Then I moved on to the nut graph before describing the benefits of being more grateful, using the Isacson family as an example. The story structure is similar to the first piece, but I included the Isacson anecdote and used different quotes from Dr. Uswatte for this story. Because of the tight word count limitations, I didn't include Emmons' quotes. But the bottom line is that the two stories, while they were on a very similar subject, were in no way identical. That's essential for effective reslanting.

Here's the piece for the *Trib*:

Kelly James-Enger 623 words
[contact info] Rights per contract

The Gift of Gratitude

by

Kelly James-Enger

As the mom of a two-year-old, I've been working on teaching my son manners. He knows how to sign "thank you" and can say it, but I have to remind him to do so. [Very brief lead.]

In fact, children aren't born with an innate desire to express thanks—as parents, we teach it to them. But it turns out that gratitude may be more than just good manners. New research shows that it can provide both emotional as well as physical health benefits. [Nut graph.]

But gratitude encompasses more than simply appreciating something that's happened, says Gitendra Uswatte, Ph.D., assistant professor of psychology at the University of Alabama at Birmingham. "We [researchers] don't think of gratitude as simply saying 'thank you,' or of being appreciative," says Uswatte. "It's an emotion that reflects thankfulness for benefits received from other individuals, nature, or a higher being," he says. [Definition of gratitude, according to researchers.]

In a study published last year, Uswatte and his coauthors studied two groups of Vietnam War veterans: those with post-traumatic stress disorder and those without. While on average, veterans with PTSD had lower levels of gratitude than vets without PTSD, those who expressed gratitude more often reported higher levels of life satisfaction than others. In another study, participants who regularly listed five things they were grateful for felt better about their lives and had fewer physical complaints than people who listed five neutral events. [Describing the research about gratitude.]

Yet adults and children alike tend to take the good things in our life for granted—or to focus on what we don't have. Teaching your children to be more appreciative can help give them a different perspective on what we *do* have, says Uswatte.

Heather Isacson, a mom of four children ages 23 months to 10 years, says it's important for her children to feel—and express—gratitude. "In our family, [gratitude] is to be thankful for what we have, and to make our children understand the difference between needs and wants...and not to forget about things that we have that other people don't have," says Isacson, of Downers Grove. That attitude extends to saying thanks—in addition to sending thank-you notes for gifts, her older children write personal notes to their sports coaches at the end of the season. [See how Isacson's anecdote supports the concept behind the story?]

In addition, while they do get gifts from relatives, the Isacsons don't ask for gifts from other kids at their birthday parties; instead guests are asked to bring something that can be donated to needy families. For example, for Noah's August birthday, he asked his guests to bring school supplies which he helps his mom deliver to Sharing Connections [a local charity] and local schools. Clay, 8, celebrates his birthday in January, and has had guests bring mittens, hats and gloves for people who need them. [Another anecdote aimed at parents reading the piece.]

So what can you do to encourage your kids to be more grateful? Simply asking your child, "What good things happened to you today?" is an easy way to start, says Uswatte. That helps your child focus on the positive aspects of his or her life.

Of course, as a parent you're a role model, and if you're appreciative of others, your children are likely to follow in your example. Help your young kids write thank-you notes, and explain that thanking the gift-giver makes that person feel happy. Make it a point to say "thank you" more often and your children will, too. [More advice for parents.]

Your efforts are likely to go beyond producing well-mannered children. "Consider the research showing that this is a strength that is strongly linked to life satisfaction, so adults who are high in gratitude tend to be highly satisfied with their lives," he says. "For most parents, their strongest wish is for their child to be happy—and this is a quality that's been strongly linked to happiness." [Simple but strong close.]

-30-

Step 6: Turn both stories in.
I turned in both stories, along with my backup material. Both editors were happy with the articles, and accepted them.

Step 7: Get both clips, and get paid.
My story in the *Trib* ran a couple of weeks later; the custom magazine piece, four months later. As usual, I let my sources know. And I was paid by both markets within three weeks of turning in both pieces. Nice!

In this chapter, you've learned how to approach longer, multi-source articles. Can you see that the process isn't any different from writing short, one-source stories? Now let's look at some other types of articles you may pitch and write in chapter 9.

CHAPTER 9:
Expand your Repertoire: Writing Other Types of Articles

In the last two chapters, you've seen how to approach both short pieces and longer stories. Now let's take a look at some specific types of articles you may write.

The Profile

The profile is a staple of nearly every publication. While a profile is usually of a person, sometimes markets will profile a business or nonprofit organization. In every case, you should consider the subject of the story and the market you're writing for when pitching and writing a profile.

So when I wrote a profile of a soap opera actress for a fitness magazine, the piece addressed her fitness regime and diet in addition to her acting career and personal life. A profile about a fourth generation grocery store owner for *IGA Grocergram* focused on how she had grown up in the business and her transition from "daughter of the boss" to store owner. And the below story about a professional athlete for a diabetes magazine included how she manages her diabetes and how it affects her career.

One-source profiles rely on one interview, almost always with the person being featured. With longer or more complex profiles, you may interview other sources, typically people who know the person well, have worked with him or her, or who have background information about the source that the person himself may not offer (or even want to talk about).

While celebrity magazines, websites, and blogs often feature lots of "unnamed sources" and "sources close to" the subject of the story, expect to have to name names to your editor when you turn a piece in. So let's look at a sample profile and how I approached the reporting and writing of the piece.

Step 1: Get the assignment.

I was doing some work for a custom magazine for people with diabetes. My editor asked if I was willing to write a profile of Michelle McGann, a pro golfer who also happened to have diabetes. We agreed to a rate of $0.75/word for an 1,100-word piece.

I asked whether he had already been in contact with McGann or her publicist. He had, which made it easy to contact McGann directly to arrange an interview.

If you're writing about a celebrity or other well-know person, you may have to do a little extra legwork to figure out who you should contact. If I don't have a lead, I start with Google and try the person's name and go from there; I can often find the appropriate person (whether a manager or PR rep) through the person's website. There are also websites like www.whorepresents.com (that stands for "who represents") that you can use to locate the names and contact info for celebrities' managers and agents.

The more well-known and in demand a person is, the more hoops you can expect to jump through. You'll have to tell your contact the name of the market you're writing for, the nature of the story, and the angle you plan to take, and may have to submit questions ahead of time for approval. In many cases, the subject's PR person will want to be involved with the interview, even if only to be on the call.

Step 2: Research the story.

However, in this case, I emailed McGann directly to arrange the interview, and told her to expect that it would take 30 to 40 minutes. Ordinarily my interviews are fairly short, but for a profile, expect to spend at least a half hour to an hour on the phone. (I personally wouldn't use email for a profile interview as it takes away the immediacy and freshness of a phone or in-person interview. You can, however, follow up with a few questions via email if you forgot to ask about something important.)

I did some background research on McGann before I interviewed her so I wouldn't waste time asking her about recent LPGA wins, her date of birth, and the like. That research also lets me conduct a better interview. Not only will I make the most of my interview time; if she can tell I've done my homework ahead of time, she's likely to give me a better interview, remember?

One of my freelance friends who has interviewed dozens of celebrities uses this technique as well. She'll do some in-depth reporting before she speaks to the celebrity, and at the beginning of the interview, is sure to ask a question that reflects her knowledge of the star's career. That always results in better quotes, which means she writes better stories.

Step 3: Conduct the interview.

My interview with McCann went well; the transcript appears below. As with any interview, I may chat with my source for a minute or two to break the ice, but I don't bother to transcribe that.

Michelle McGann
[contact info omitted]

[When were you diagnosed with diabetes? How did it happen?] I was 13 years old, my mom is a nurse and she was actually away on a seminar on diabetes and came home and I'd lost a ton of weight, and told my dad, Michelle's diabetic, he thought she was crazy, you're a pediatric nurse, you work with them all the time, went in the next day and sure enough I have every symptom imaginable, I went on an experimental program in London, Ontario about four or five weeks after I was diagnosed and was on insulin

didn't know is this going to work, is this going to not work, whatever, the doctors said take a chance and see what happens, we did that, and I was off insulin five years, as a result of that it was great, but it became too toxic to your kidneys

[were you scared?]

the thing, I didn't have a clue what it was, I was athletic, I played golf and sports, and softball, and didn't have a clue what it meant, then I started learning about it and can I play sports and I can't have Mountain Dew and now you can find almost everything that's sugar-free, but then I didn't really have an idea of what it was about, and I went to Canada once a month for five years so it was all kind of like I've got a lot going on

[How was your family during this time?]

My family was supportive and behind me and helping me, and my mom being a nurse helped a great deal as well but for any kid it's scary, when I talk to kids out on tour and people that you run into throughout your travels, it's amazing how many young kids come up to you, and say I have diabetes and what can you tell me, you try to make them try to feel easy about it and you can handle it and it's no big deal, you can easily manage it, and do all the right things and you'll be good to go

[I read that you started golfing at eight. How did your diagnosis impact your game?]

I was very serious about golf and that was like what happens now can I keep playing with this disease, really if you don't know somebody who has it, there's really no reason why you would know anything about it, it's a very common disease but unless you bring it up to someone they would have no idea of how you look or the way you act, when your blood sugar it gets too low, you act a little stupider, a little goofy just because it gets so low your mind and body is not functioning like it should be but there's no other way someone would know...

The five years that I was off insulin, that was a treat, to have the ability to not have to have to take shots all the time when you eat and have a little more freer schedule, when I went back on insulin, it was a little tougher, just because the peaks and the valleys trying to figure out I got to eat and I've got to tee off, I've got to take insulin and there were times when you didn't think enough and got in big trouble, this is my third year on the insulin pump, it's been unbelievable, night and day

[Tell me more about how the pump has affected your performance]

for instance when I was on insulin, how it affects your game, I was leading the US Open at Crooked Stick in 1996 or 1995, and maybe earlier, had an insulin reaction, had eaten pasta, before I went out, and had a late tee time, all of a sudden I didn't know where I was and that were uncharacteristic of how I had been playing and it took me four or five holes to get my blood sugar back up and then I ended up playing better, but when the adrenaline is pumping, I don't care what sport you're in, you don't want to eat and that's probably one of the toughest things you deal with, people ask me all the time what I eat when I play, I can't seem to keep my blood sugar high enough, and it's like well, it's not the easiest thing to keep up but being on the pump, night and day as far as the flexibility of being able to work out, you can regulate how much insulin you get every hour, if you want to work out hard doing aerobic exercise, you can turn it down so you don't have a 40 or 50 blood sugar an hour later...whereas you can turn it down, everybody's body reacts a little differently to exercise, the best thing is I can turn it down and when I finish exercising, I've got a 120, a normal range blood sugar instead of dealing with 40 or 50 where you can't get enough in your mouth, and it's the worst feeling ever, it's wonderful in that aspect, as far as getting up in the morning, you don't have to be on such a rigid schedule, you have to get up at 7 or at 8, because your body's getting insulin, but on a normal basis, you can have a flexible lunch, you can skip right over it, you're getting insulin to keep your body regulated during the day, can eat at 2 if you want, and playing golf is extremely great, tee off at 9 and 10:30 or 11 you're making the turn and you're hungry, so you can eat a sandwich then, and then you can finish and eat then , it's so much easier than oh, I have to eat something every couple of holes, you don't have to worry about it

it's so much easier with the pump, it's not perfect, people say oh you're on the pump, everything is wonderful, well this disease is not perfect, you can be on the pump, you can be on insulin shots and I don't care if it's you can have days where you think I did the same thing as yesterday and for some reason my blood sugar is sugar is higher today doing the same exact thing, that's the tough part about it, you can't say you're going to get it perfect because you really can't, I've asked my doctor why does it happen, some days it's a little higher, your emotions affect it, the adrenaline, when you're fired up and you're competing, the weather the heat and the cold, both affect my blood sugar differently, but the nice thing is if you do have an elevated blood sugar, you can correct it by pushing a few buttons on the pump instead of taking a shot and overlapping and then you start getting really crazy,

so many great things about the traveling, traveling overseas, you can change the time on the pump your body is constantly getting insulin so your body doesn't get screwed up is you were taking shots four or five or six times a day

[Golf is such a mental sport. How do you maintain your focus?]

I think a lot of that has to do with it, you get in the zone, you compete and you do it on a regular basis, it becomes part of your routine and part of your thought process, thinking out shots, makes you mentally concentrate on what you're doing for me, the adrenaline, you try to keep an even keel, try not to get too high or too low, try to keep that steady base, that's what has worked for me, I honestly haven't come off a golf course real high or after an emotional round, it hasn't affected my blood sugar that much which is a good thing, but you love to compete and you love to play and you practice certain things and the mental side is a big part of it, you just try to keep things in perspective, not too high and not too low, keep an even keel and keep everything in perspective, not too

[What's your training schedule like?]

This last off season has been the longest I've had in the 13 years of my career so I've had the opportunity to work quite a bit with my trainer, I'd say 2 to 4 times a week depending on our schedules, set up a routine I try to do 4 times a week with or without him at least half of the time he's there, leg weights and upper body weights, and usually about 25 minutes before , I ride the bike or walk on the treadmill, do a lot of stretching before and during and after, then I'll usually get on the bike or treadmill again for another 15 or 20 minutes to keep the muscles in tone and not tighten up too much, probably about an hour and 45 minutes, somewhere in there give or take

In the off season, probably anywhere from 4 to 6 hours depending on whether I've played or just practicing or if I'm just hitting balls or working on my short game and putting probably only about 3, can't stand there forever, the PGA National is the course I represent, and the health club is right on the property, so I leave here in the morning and have golf clothes on and I practice and then the workout clothes are in a duffle bag so if I do a little later in the day, I'll practice until dark, and go to the health club and usually I'm home by 8 or so

[Your brother is no longer going to caddy for you. Who's replacing him?]

My dad just had knee surgery and my brother is back in Florida State, finishing up his last year, I'm sure I'm going to miss it, this is the first year I wont' have, last year my brother did quite a bit, my dad hasn't done so much because my brother had but they'll still come out and follow me and one of my close friends is going to caddy for it, we kind of have that brother/sister relationship as well, we grew up together and he's a little bit older than me so I think we've got a good combination of both of our personalities and the drive to compete and positive attitude which is half the battle as well so I think it's going to be a good combination

[Tell me about your line of hats]

Just this year I have my own line of clothes and hats, it's the Michelle McGann Collection, it's about a month and a half later coming out now, I'm waiting for my shirts to arrive…it will be out this year to all the clubs, throughout the country, it's 6 colors, black white pink green yellow and blue and there are going to be three patterns to start off with and throughout the year will be additional ones, very fun, capris, skirt, 2 different style of shorts and a skort, 4 different shirts and sweaters and a cotton twill sweatshirt, and there will be straw hats to match and ball caps, there is going to be belts, socks, it's a whole collection and hopefully I'll have most of that out on tour within the next month

[Do you do any spokesperson work?]

I represent Cadillac, there are only three of us that wear the logo Freddy Couples and Tom Watson and myself, and I represent Minimed, hopefully that's going to continue...that's probably one of my biggest, obviously I live with this disease and I feel very strongly about the pump, all the positive things it has to offer everyone, of course we all can't wait to see a cure

[What would say to someone recently diagnosed?]

I think the biggest thing is that it is a disease that is manageable, you don't have any limits on your potential to do anything, you can do it, and I guess you're control your own destiny, it's real simple, you manage it, you take control of your own body and if you work hard, I think I've proven a lot of that, I've traveled all over the world it, and I've won many golf tournaments and I've worked hard at it, despite having a disease I don't know how many millions of people have

[How do you maintain the motivation to keep playing year after year?]

This was the 13th year that I just finished, so the break came at a very good time, it is tough, I've had some really great years and a couple not so great not that I've fallen to rock bottom by any means, at least not what I expected and I think a lot of it is confidence and when I lost a little bit of confidence, it was very difficult to drive and drive to get back, as hard as you drive, the one little bit of luck that could have gone your way went the other way, sometimes it's difficult to explain that to people, golf is such a difficult game anyway, when you're competing at our level you need to have some of that little luck on your side and you need to run with it when it comes there, sometimes I think I have a tendency to get too down, after everything that happened on the 11th and a friend of our passed away in her early 30s of diabetes and was going in for a kidney transplant and passed away a couple of days before it, so I think that seeing all that and all the work her family has put into the research institute, different things motivate everybody, but I've just decided that this is going to be one of my best years and I have so many positive things going in my direction, and I think if you talk to any athlete, what's your main drive, first you want to be the best there is but you have to have the support and the background to be your best, as much as we like to think that you can do a lot of stuff on your own, you've got to have that friend that you call and say you shot 65 today and they're just as fired up as you are and when you say you shot 72, they say it's no big deal, you need to have good solid people behind you, and I think I have a great foundation, they're all fired up as I am to get out there and play and you take a lot of good energy with you and the confidence keeps getting greater and greater the xxx are going in and then things are going to change a bit...

[What are your goals for the future?]

I'm just trying to get back to the top in the next 2, 3 or 4, years, I really haven't thought about what I might like to do, I love to do corporate work, I also represent Bayer, they have the Dex 2 is the new blood sugar machine, and I'm using that, doing corporate work with them and with Cadillac, and interacting with people and doing clinics, you'd be amazed this isn't a microphone on my belt, this isn't a beeper before anyone starts out and has you know is that a mike, you have to explain and you'd be amazed at how many people by the end of that day come up to me and say you know what I have diabetes, tell me about it, or my granddaughter, or my son or my wife, unbelievable the can of worms that that opens up and I feel that probably I will get a lot more involved in doing more corporate stuff and doing things that I can pass, hey listen I'm a successful professional athlete and this is what I've done and this is one of the reasons I'm as good as I am, and educate people because that's the biggest things, people lack and they just don't' know so they assume and most of the time they assume wrong, so I really do enjoy doing that kind of stuff

Step 4: Write the Piece

I find profiles hard to write. You're trying to encapsulate someone's life in just a few hundred words! How am I possibly supposed to do that? So I kept my two questions in mind—who are my readers, and what will they want to know about Michelle McGann.

I read through my transcript several times and made notes about the information I knew I wanted to include in the piece—her diagnosis and how she's managed her diabetes; her success on the golf course; and her future plans. Then I thought about how to approach the lead. I decided to use a general lead designed to (hopefully) draw readers in to the story.

Here's the piece I submitted, with my comments in brackets:

Kelly James-Enger   1,137 words
[contact info]   Rights per written contract

Michelle McGann:

Dedicated, Down-to-Earth, and Driven to Succeed

by

Kelly James-Enger

Ask any golfer and he or she will probably admit to fantasizing about playing as a pro. What could be better than spending sunny days out on the golf course, getting paid to do something you love?

The reality is that professional golfers, like any athletes, put in long hours both on and off the course year-round. Succeeding in this competitive arena requires more than love of the game—it takes talent, commitment, mental strength, and tremendous drive. [This lead contrasts the reader's fantasy—playing golf for a living—with the reality of what it entails.]

Golfer Michelle McGann has all these qualities. As a member of the Ladies Professional Golf Association ("LPGA") Tour for thirteen years, she has turned a childhood love for golf into her fulltime career—and she's done it all while having to manage her diabetes as well. Yet McGann has never used her diabetes as an excuse—it's simply one more factor to take into account as she practices and competes. [I introduce Michelle McGann, who readers may not have heard of. Yet they'll presumably be interested in her story, because like them, she's dealing with diabetes.]

Growing up, McGann was a natural athlete who enjoyed playing softball and other sports in addition to golfing. It was her mother, a nurse, who realized that she had the classic symptoms of diabetes at thirteen. A doctor's visit confirmed her suspicion.

McGann, who had started golfing at eight years old, remembers being worried about what her diagnosis meant for her golfing career. She wasn't sure whether she'd be able to continue playing. "I didn't have a clue what it [diabetes] was," says McGann. "My mom being a nurse helped a great deal, but for any kid, it's scary." [Background on McGann, along with a direct quote so we know what she was experiencing.]

After a few weeks on insulin, McGann took part in an experimental treatment for diabetes that required monthly visits to London, Ontario. While the treatment worked for five years, it eventually became too toxic to her kidneys and she had to go back on insulin. That meant she had to continually adjust her insulin and try to maintain good control during tournaments. For her, as with anyone with diabetes, it's been a learning process.

"For instance, I was leading the US Open at Crooked Stick one year and I had an insulin reaction," remembers McGann. "All of a sudden I didn't know where I was and I was making shots that were uncharacteristic of how I had been playing. It took me four or five holes to get my blood sugar back up and then I ended up playing better. That [fluctuation in blood sugar] is probably one of the toughest things you deal with." [More background, and more quotes from her about how diabetes affects her.]

McGann has been on the insulin pump for three years. While she still monitors her blood sugar carefully, she says the pump has made practicing and playing much easier. "You're getting insulin to keep your body regulated during the day," she says. "You can tee off at 9, and at 10:30 or 11, you're making the turn [golfing term—I should have explained what this means] and you're hungry, so you can eat a sandwich—and then you can finish playing and eat. It's so much easier than, 'Oh, I have to eat something every couple of holes.' You don't have to worry about it."

Golf is known as a mental game, and McGann has to be able to maintain her focus throughout tournaments. She says that regular playing helps hone her concentration skills on the course. "You compete on a regular basis, and it becomes part of your routine and part of your thought process," she says. "Thinking out shots makes you mentally concentrate on what you're doing... you try to keep an even keel, try not to get too high or too low—that's what has worked for me." [Note that I'm using lots of direct quotes. I want readers to feel like McGann's talking to them.]

While she tries to keep things in perspective, it can be tough. McGann has had some stellar years—she won tournaments in 95, 96, and 97—but the past few years she hasn't fared as well. "I've had some really great years and a couple not so great—not that I've fallen to rock bottom by any means, but at least not what I expected," says McGann. "I think a lot of it is confidence and when I lost a little bit of confidence, it was very difficult to drive and drive to get back."

While fans may only see golfers out on the course during the season, McGann trains from her home in Florida during winter months as well. She performs a workout that includes cardio work, strength training and stretching two to four times a week. And she spends about 4 to 6 hours a day playing and practicing at the PGA National Golf Course in West Palm Beach.

McGann has maintained a close relationship with her family, and this will be the first year that her dad or her brother will not be caddying for her. Her dad recently had knee surgery and her younger brother is finishing his last year at Florida State University. "I'm sure I'm going to miss it...but they'll still come out and follow me," says McGann. She's happy that one of her close friends has agreed to caddy for her this year. [More background about McGann.]

"You have to have the support and the background to be your best," she explains. "You need to have good solid people behind you, and I think I have a great foundation. They're all as fired up as I am to get out there and play." [McGann reflecting on the importance of family support. I like her direct quotes here.]

McGann, who's well-known not only for her prowess on the course but for her signature hats and outfits, has launched a clothing line as well. The Michelle McGann Collection includes golf wear in a variety of colors with matching straw hats and ball caps and accessories like belts and socks. She'd excited about the line of clothes, which will be available at golf clubs throughout the country. She also acts as a spokesperson for Cadillac, and MiniMed, the company that makes her insulin pump. [Background on her other ventures.]

But her current focus is on the coming golf season. McGann recently lost a close friend to diabetes and says that that event and the attacks of

September 11 have motivated her to play at the top of her game. "Different things motivate everybody, but I've just decided that this is going to be one of my best years," she says. "I have so many positive things going in my direction ... and I'm just trying to get back to the top in the next two, three, or four years." [What keeps her motivated.]

She's aware too of the positive influence she can have on people, especially children, who have diabetes. "It's amazing how many young kids come up to you, and say, 'I have diabetes and what can you tell me?'" she says. "You try to make them try to feel easy about it and tell them 'you can handle it and it's no big deal...do all the right things and you'll be good to go.' I think the biggest thing [for people to know] is that it is a disease that is manageable. You don't have any limits on your potential to do anything." [Uplifting close, especially important for the readers of this publication.]

-30-

Step 5: Turn the piece in.

As I reread this story, about ten years after writing it, I realize it's not a stellar profile. I could have used stronger imagery, and interviewed someone else (maybe her mother, or another LPGA member) to add depth to the profile. But my editor was happy with it. My point is that when I look at anything I wrote years ago—queries, essays, articles, even books—I always know that today I could do a better job. That's because the more you write, the better you become at it. You'll find this to be the case, too.

Step 6: Get paid.

I received my check for $825 about a month later.

Step 7: Get my clip.

When the story was published, my editor sent several copies to McGann. Otherwise, I would have done the same for her.

The Quiz Article

Writing a story that incorporates a quiz is an easy way to engage and educate readers, and they're particularly popular with online markets because of their interactive aspect. I've written dozens of quizzes on topics ranging from psychology ("How Much of a Perfectionist are You?") to finances ("What's Your Money Personality?") to nutrition ("Test your Food IQ") to fitness ("What are your Workout Roadblocks?"). I even wrote an article on how to write quizzes that used a quiz as its lead. Clever, huh?

First step of pitching and writing a quiz story is to identify the subject matter you're writing about, and how the quiz will work in the piece. Will it be the entire story, a lead, or a sidebar? Any of those three options can work. Then decide on the quiz format itself. Will it be multiple choice? True/false? Will readers be able to "score" their results at the end?

To write a compelling quiz, you'll need to know the subject matter you're writing about. I've always been able to write my questions and answers from my background research and interviews, but I make sure that I have the quiz format in mind as I'm conducting my interviews. Then I refer to my notes as I craft the quiz itself.

So, for example, for a story on "money personalities," I wrote a quiz that let readers determine which type of personality they had. In that case, my source, psychologist Linda Barbanel, the author of *Sex, Money and Power*, had identified and described four major "money styles" in her book. After interviewing her about them, I wrote questions that would help readers determine which type they were. I had already decided that each "A" answer would be the "Keeper" response; each "B" would be the "Power Seeker;" each "C," the "Love Buyer;" and each "D," the "Freedom Searcher."

Here are some of the questions I included in the quiz:

1. You just won $500 in a raffle. You:
A. Stash it in the bank.
B. Invest in a few shares of a hot new stock.
C. Spend it on your family.
D. Splurge on a weekend trip.
2. Growing up, your parents:
A. Often worried about making ends meet.
B. Didn't consult each other about financial decisions.
C. Rewarded you for good grades or behavior.
D. Never really talked about money.
3. Children should have an allowance because:
A. It lets them start saving early.
B. It teaches them the value of money.
C. They should be able to buy things for themselves.
D. It lets them make independent spending decisions.
4. You use credit cards:
A. For emergencies only.
B. Frequently for business and entertaining.
C. To buy things you want for yourself or your family.
D. Most when travelling.
5. The birthday gift you'd most enjoy:
A. Something practical.
B. A hard-to-find, top-of-the-line watch.
C. An expensive dinner out.

D. A gift certificate from your favorite store.

After the quiz questions, I included the line, "If you answered mostly As, you're a "Keeper;" mostly Bs, you're a "Power Seeker;" mostly Cs, a "Love Buyer;" and mostly Ds, a "Freedom Searcher." The main story had defined the money styles and given advice for each specific type.

Get the idea? If you're writing a quiz that lets a reader test his or her knowledge of a subject, remember to include the correct answer at the end. If you've ever taken an online quiz, you've already seen how this works. So let's walk through the process:

Step 1: Pitch the idea.

I queried a women's magazine with my idea, which was overcoming common nutrition mistakes.

Step 2: Get the assignment.

While my editor liked the idea, she asked me to reslant it a bit to focus on nutrition myths, not nutrition mistakes. I'd written for the market before so the contract wasn't an issue, and I'd be paid $0.75/word for an 1,100-word piece.

Step 3: Confirm the topic.

Before I started writing the piece, my editor asked me to come up with fifteen nutrition myths I'd be debunking. I emailed her suggestions, and then tweaked the list based on her feedback. If you're a new writer, your editor may ask you to do something similar, or provide a brief outline before you write the piece. No big deal—she's only making sure the two of you are on the same page.

Step 4: Research the piece.

I reached out to several nutrition experts I had spoken with before, and conducted interviews with them. (I don't interview a source more than once every year or so, but I do like to "return to the well," so to speak, when I have a source who's smart, informed, and quotable. Better yet, former sources remember me because I'm such a delight. Or because I send thank-yous and let them know when they're quoted. I realize it's the latter.)

Step 5: Write the piece.

This was a fun, easy piece to write. Using my notes from my interviews (I'd asked sources about the nutrition myths I'd identified and the truth behind them), I constructed the piece. Note that I don't have to attribute every answer to an expert, but when I turn in my fact-checking material, I'll indicate which source gave me each piece of information.

Here's the story. This ran in a print mag but could just have easily been written for a Website:

Kelly James-Enger   1,121 words
[contact info]   First rights

Test your Nutritional IQ

By

Kelly James-Enger

Have you ever bragged about how clean your diet is? Do friends rely on your nutritional savvy when they have questions about healthy foods? Or do you know how you *should* be eating but find it takes too much effort? [Simple lead.]

Test your nutritional know-how by answering the questions below:

1. If you're planning on having a big dinner, skipping breakfast will let you save up calories so you don't gain weight as a result.
2. Drinking eight eight-ounce glasses of water will keep you hydrated.
3. It's difficult for vegetarians to consume enough protein.
4. "No-fat" foods are better for you than regular-fat versions.
5. You should eat five servings of fruits and vegetables for optimal health.
6. Nuts are bad for you because they're high in fat.
7. Eating foods low on the glycemic index can help you lose weight.
8. "Whole wheat" and "whole grain" bread are the same things.
9. High-fiber foods can help you lose weight.
10. If you eat a high-protein diet, you're more likely to become dehydrated.
11. The best mid-day snack is something high in carbs like a bagel or pretzels.
12. Because they're high in calories, beans should be eaten only rarely.
13. Eating out frequently can cause weight gain.
14. Beer is a good source of carbohydrates.
15. Negative calorie foods like celery help you lose weight.

[Now we get into the meat of the story, debunking some nutrition myths.]

1. False. It seems logical that the fewer calories you eat for breakfast and lunch, the more you can afford to consume later on. But when you undereat during the day, you set yourself up for overeating at dinner, says American Dietetic Association spokesperson Jackie Berning, an assistant professor of nutrition at the University of Colorado at Colorado Springs. Better bet: spread your calories evenly throughout the day. [I identify one of my sources.]

2. False. The standard of 8 eight-ounce glasses of water is only a guideline. For some people, this may be a sufficient amount of H2o—but if you exercise intensely, it may not be nearly enough. Consider this—according to the American College of Sports Medicine, people should drink 14 to 22 ounces of fluid 2 to 3 hours before exercise; 6 to 12 ounces of fluid every 15 to 20 minutes during exercise; and 16 to 24 ounces of fluid for every pound of body weight lost during exercise. [This fact came from a special report of the ACSM. I included the URL when I turned in the piece for fact-checking.]

3. False. While vegans—people who don't eat any animal products—may have a difficult time consuming enough protein, vegetarians who eat eggs and dairy products have no trouble. Soy products, nuts, beans, and foods made with "TVP" (texturized vegetable protein) can all contribute to your protein needs as well. [Note that each answer provides readers with helpful nutrition info.]

4. False. Many no-fat or low-fat foods have as many calories as the original versions. But because the fat has been reduced or eliminated, eating these foods may not give the same feeling

of satisfaction or fullness. Worse yet, there's more of a temptation to go overboard, rationalizing "it's fat-free." Remember, calories still count.

5. False. Five servings a day is a great start, but studies show that eating even more fruits and vegetables can produce additional health benefits such as reducing your risk of cardiovascular disease. "Fruits and vegetables tend to be lower in calories and more jam-packed with vitamins and minerals than other foods," says Berning. The more you eat, the less you'll consume of more calorie-dense foods, which can help you lose or maintain your weight.

6. False. Forget the idea that nuts or any other food is "bad." Nuts do contain fat, but they're also a good source of protein as well. This doesn't mean you have *carte blanche* to inhale the cashews, but they fit into a healthy diet.

7. True. Research suggests that lower GI foods—which enter the bloodstream more slowly—produce less dramatic blood sugar peaks and valleys, which may even out hunger levels and reduce food cravings. [I'll need a study to confirm this, or have one of my experts state this is the case in their transcripts.]

8. False. Food packages can be tricky—"whole wheat" bread may have been processed and had caramel coloring added to look like whole wheat. To be classified as "whole grain," however, the food has to contain all three parts of the grain kernel including the bran, or outer coating, the germ, and the endosperm.

9. True. Research bears this out. Fiber helps fill you up, so you wind up eating less. Studies have found that increasing fiber intake is associated with lower overall caloric intake. Shoot for 25 to 30 grams a day. [I'll need to have a study to support this, or have

one of my experts back up this claim.]

10. True. In a recent study, athletes who increased their protein intake to about 30% of their total calories had more concentrated urine as a result, which could lead to dehydration. Make sure you're eating an appropriate amount of protein for your body weight and activity level, and always drink plenty of fluids. [I don't say where the "recent study" was published, but I'll need to have a copy of it to turn in for fact-checking.]

11. False. Add protein or fat to your carbohydrate snack, and it will have more staying power. "Combining carbohydrates with protein and or fat helps slow down the absorption of carbohydrates, which are digested and absorbed rapidly," explains Susan M. Kleiner, Ph.D., author of *Power Eating, The Second Edition* (Human Kinetics, 2001). So put a little peanut butter on your apple slices or add some turkey or light cream cheese to your bagel. [Again, I don't just debunk the myth—I give readers tips to help them eat better.]

12. False. Beans are calorically dense but they're also a low-fat, high-protein food that contain phytochemicals and soluble fiber, which has been shown to reduce your risk of cardiovascular disease. Make them a regular part of your diet.

13. True. Blame the portions—a recent survey found that restaurant portions are often three to four sizes larger than standard ones. And not surprisingly, another study found that women who eat fast food frequently are more likely to weigh more—and gain weight—than women who pass up the burgers and fries. [Here we go with more studies. No problem, but I'll need copies of them to back up these claims.]

14. False. "People may think that beer is a good source of

carbohydrates, but alcohol carbohydrate is different than other carbohydrates," says Berning. Carbohydrates from food are digested and absorbed by your body while carbs from alcohol go straight to the liver, where they're broken down. Alcohol in moderation is fine, but forget about "carbo-loading" with a six-pack! [This in an informative article, but the tone is light, to match the market.]

15. False. "There is no such thing as a 'negative calorie food'," says Berning. "As long it's providing energy, it contains calories." While 10 to 15% of the total calories of any food will be used to digest and metabolize it, the rest will be available to your body.

So, how'd you do? If you got 13-15 correct, you're a master of nutrition; 10-12 correct, you're well-educated about nutrition but still fall for some myths; 6-9 correct, you're about average when it comes to nutritional know-how; and less than 5 correct, you need to brush up on the facts—not myths—about the food you eat! [I made up this scoring tally, by the way. But my editor liked it, which is all I care about.]

-30-

Step 6: Turn in the piece.

I turned in the story, along with my fact-checking info, to my editor. I mentioned earlier that I like to submit a second copy of the article, with notes indicating where facts and quotes came from. Here's what a couple of paragraphs from the above story would look like:

1. False. It seems logical that the fewer calories you eat for breakfast and lunch, the more you can afford to consume later on. But when you undereat during the day, you set yourself up for overeating at dinner, says American Dietetic Association spokesperson Jackie Berning, an assistant professor of nutrition at the University of Colorado at Colorado Springs. Better bet: spread your calories evenly throughout the day. [From Jackie

Berning, and I provide her contact info.]

2. False. The standard of 8 eight-ounce glasses of water is only a guideline. For some people, this may be a sufficient amount of H2o—but if you exercise intensely, it may not be nearly enough. Consider this—according to the American College of Sports Medicine, people should drink 14 to 22 ounces of fluid 2 to 3 hours before exercise; 6 to 12 ounces of fluid every 15 to 20 minutes during exercise; and 16 to 24 ounces of fluid for every pound of body weight lost during exercise. ["ACSM Special Report on Hydration," I include the URL to the report if it's available online or a copy of the report itself. I'd do the same thing with a journal article or other statistic or fact that didn't come from one of my interviews.]

If you turn in a story with a lot of backup material—say, a half-dozen journal articles—I suggest you label each of them as "A," "B," etc. Then on your annotated copy, you can write, "See article, attached as 'A.'" Make it easy for your editor, or her fact-checker, to do her job.

Step 7: Get paid.

Got my check for $825 in less than two weeks! Love that.

Step 8: Get my clip.

Five months later, I got my copy of the magazine in the mail and notified my sources that they were quoted.

The Round-Up Article

Editors love round-ups. Most freelancers, not so much. So if starting out, why not pitch and write some? They take time to research but are simple to write.

So, what's a round-up? It's usually a list of sorts, often of short quotes by a number of different sources. The subject matter depends on the market. Here's how I approached a round-up for a fitness publication:

Step 1: Get the assignment.

My editor emailed to ask if I could do a roundup piece for her. She wanted me to interview women on a Chicago beach about their workout regimes. Even though ordinarily I do all of my research and reporting from my desk, I agreed to go "on location" for the piece. I'd be paid $0.75/word for 450 words.

Step 2: Hit the beach!

I took the train into Chicago from my suburban home, and met up with a freelance photographer and his lighting guy. Then we eyeballed attractive, twenty-something, fit-looking women to decide who we should approach. Believe me, I felt like a stalker. As the writer (and lone female in our trio), it was my job to walk up to these women and ask if we could A. take their picture and B. run it in a national magazine. It wasn't my favorite assignment, although it only took a couple of hours to get what I needed. (For the record, only two women refused. Everyone else was flattered and delighted to be included!)

I took notes as we interviewed each woman, and the photographer shot them. Less than two hours later, I was on my way home, writing the piece on the train.

Step 3: Write the piece.

This story was a cinch to write. Here it is:

Kelly James-Enger   451 Words
[Contact info]   First N.A. rights

Getting Fit in Chicago

By

Kelly James-Enger

In Chicago, one of the best places to run, walk, bike or 'blade is along Lake Michigan. We hung out at North Avenue Beach one Saturday to find out what brought them to the beach—and how these "Windy City" babes keep fit:

"I'm running the marathon this year so I alternate walking and running—today I'm walking. I've run some half-marathons, but I've never run a marathon before. I'm doing about 25 to 30 miles a week right now—the longest we've run so far is nine miles. I usually go to the gym and lift three times a week, too." Jill, 25

"I'm here to play volleyball—I've been playing for 6 years and usually play once or twice a week. I'm in a league that plays on Wednesday nights and I also go to the gym about twice a week and lift weights and run." Leslie, 30

"I usually run along here—I run five times week, between three and ten miles a day. I may be doing the marathon this year—I'm on target for it, but that's supposed to be a secret! I also swim once in a while and rollerblade five or six miles at least three times a week." Laura, 23

"I'm from Milwaukee and this is my first time here for beach Spinning—a friend inspired me to come. I'm a triathlete and I work out every day—I swim, bike, run, and lift weights. I just placed ninth overall in a Bally's Total Fitness sprint triathlon in Milwaukee." Jennifer, 27

"I just moved to Chicago from Kansas City because my husband got transferred—I run out here but this is my first trip down to the beach. I usually run about four miles three or four times a week and lift weights every once in a while." Nikki, 27

"I'm here because we're shooting a national infomercial for an exercise video that I shot already—I have a series of seven exercise videos called G.I. Jabb. I've been a martial arts instructor for 12 years—I teach about 30 private lessons and group classes a week." Katalin, 27

"I come down here about half the time—the other half the time, I go to the gym. I work out five or six days a week—my usual routine includes running, kickboxing, lifting weights and a little Spinning." Hope, 27

"I don't come down here that often—I'm more of a gym-goer and do a lot of running on the treadmill and lifting free weights, and I take classes two or three days a week. I run, kick box and lift three or four days a week." Lauren, 23

-30-

Step 4: Turn the story in.
I turned in the piece. No edits required! Yay!
Step 5: Get my clip.
The story ran several months later, and I sent an email to all of the women I interviewed for the story to let them know about it.
Step 6: Get paid...finally.
This story was one of the last ones I did for this particular market. My original editor had left the magazine, and it was taking longer and longer to get paid. It took me nearly six months to collect payment for this story! Fortunately

I've found that to be the exception, not the rule. I will say that this was the last story I did for this magazine.

A roundup isn't always of quotes from sources. It could be a list of calorie-tracking apps to accompany a piece on weight loss, for example. A roundup can be included as a sidebar, and it's a great way to provide more information to readers that may not fit in the main story. Think of a roundup as a list and you'll find that they're easy to write once the research is done.

The Essay

While this book focuses on writing and selling nonfiction articles, I realize that many freelancers want to write essays as well. Keep in mind it's more challenging to sell an essay than an article. First, essay slots are limited; both print and online pubs buy far more articles than essays. Second, writing a compelling essay takes talent that not every writer has. One of the keys to writing a successful essay is to take something specific (i.e. an experience that you've had) and make it universal. You can't just write about what's happened to you; you have to address a larger topic that will make readers relate to the piece.

To sell an essay, you don't send a query; you write the piece, find an appropriate market for it, and send it in with a cover letter. [You'll find a cover letter example in chapter 10.]

So let's look at the process of writing and selling an essay:

Step 1: Come up with the idea.

I'd been playing around with the idea for this essay for months before I sat down to write it. When you adopt a baby, you're "expecting," but nobody knows—unless you tell them. That was the kernel of the initial idea for the piece.

Step 2: Write the essay.

One afternoon, I sat down to write the draft, and then set it aside. A week or two later, I revised it. Here's the final version:

Kelly James-Enger   700 words
[contact info]   First N.A. rights

I'm Having a Baby (Really!)

By

Kelly James-Enger

I'm having a baby.

Not that you would know it to look at me. My stomach, while not exactly flat, lacks that telltale baby bulge. But I am having a baby. I just don't know when. [Attention-getting lead. I still like this one a lot.]

My husband and I are adopting, and while the physical symptoms of pregnancy may be absent, the reality that we're going to be parents is beginning to set in. We're talking names, looking at cribs, and admiring tiny little onesies in gender-neutral shades.

But as we examine car seats and strollers and changing tables, I find I feel like an imposter. I don't have the burgeoning belly or giveaway glow that the other future mommies do. Our child isn't growing inside me. We don't even know when to expect her—or him. We just know a baby is coming. [Note the specific details in the foregoing paragraphs. Specifics are always better than generalities.]

Erik and I have endured years of well-meaning questions about whether we want kids. Well, yeah. A couple of years of trying the old-fashioned way led to fertility drugs, surgeries, and interventions that eventually culminated in five rounds of in vitro. I got pregnant several times, only to miscarry.

During those six years, we withdrew from the world. Only our closest friends knew what we were going through, but even they couldn't understand the pain we were experiencing. Why I couldn't go to a baby shower. Why I pointedly ignored pregnant women anywhere I saw them. Why I couldn't bear to even look at a baby. [The previous two paragraphs do more than give our history; they talk about the grief we were going through. And even people who haven't gone through infertility will have experienced something similar in their lives--striving for something you truly want and failing.]

Over time, my hope to carry a biological child began to dim. But my desire to be a mommy was growing stronger. For most people, pregnancy and parenthood are irretrievably linked. Others realize that giving up one needn't negate the other. I'll never carry a child or see my belly swell or feed my baby at my breast. But is that really what being a parent is about? [This paragraph actually contains the seed for at least one more essay, maybe more--what it means to be a parent. I actually wrote and sold a later piece on the traits my son Ryan has "inherited" from me, even though he's not my biological child.]

I gave up my pregnancy fantasy and focused on becoming a mom. My husband and I met with social workers, filled out reams of paperwork, and took a ten-week parenting class. We were fingerprinted, our backgrounds checked, our mental and physical health examined, our house inspected. [Again, specific details!]

We spent hours writing a "dear birth parents" letter, trying to put into words our desire to be parents, choosing photos that reflect our responsible yet fun-loving selves, promising love, time and attention, along with baby swim classes and homemade chocolate chip cookies. We started advertising. We received our license to adopt. And we waited. [Details...and an idea for another essay here, too.]

Our baby could be born any day! We knew it could happen that fast. But I couldn't share our excitement with the world. There was no swollen abdomen, no due date to circle on the calendar. Sure, we'd tried to have a baby for years. But now we really were! And yet our baby felt like a secret.

At a conference out of town, I realized people wouldn't know—unless we told them. So I started spreading the news. I announced to long-distance friends I saw only once a year, "I have big news. I'm going to be a mom!" Then I started telling business colleagues at the conference. Then I told anyone who would listen. [It's human to want to share excitement with our friends and family, whether it's about having a baby, falling in love, or getting a much-wanted job or award. Again, it's a universal emotion even if you haven't been in the shoes of a prospective adoptive parent.]

And people were thrilled. I was congratulated, hugged, blessed. I met moms, dads, aunts, and grandpas who had adopted children. I met adopted adults who told me how happy they were for me. With each good wish, each kind word, my baby became more real. I didn't realize how healing the joy I had experienced was until I got on the plane to return home. [Demonstrating the specific is also the universal--and showing how many people are impacted by adoption.]

The man sitting directly behind me was holding a newborn—six weeks, I overheard him say. When I got up, I saw him, and for the first time in years, I could look at a baby. I could admire the tiny body, the feathery eyelashes, the loosely clenched perfect fingers without feeling that awful mix of desire, jealousy, and sorrow. I gazed at this little tiny little person, utterly and completely asleep, and for the first time, I wasn't reminded of what I had lost or would never have. Instead I saw hope, and joy—and certainty. [Lots of details and I think I did a good job of describing emotions without being melodramatic.]

And I thought, *I'm* getting one of those! [I set this off as its own paragraph to make it "pop." I think it does.]

"He's beautiful," I told the baby's father, who looked up at me and smiled. And ours will be too. [The ending relates back to the lead, and gives a sense of closure.]

Step 3: Submit the piece.
I decided to send it to one of my parenting markets which had a regular essay slot, along with a brief cover letter.
Step 4: Sell the piece.
My editor loved the piece, and paid $150 for it.
Step 5: Get my clip.
The essay ran a few months later.
Step 6: Get paid.
I received my check about a week after the story ran.
Step 7: Get paid again.
This essay is another example of an "evergreen," or a story that doesn't have a "sell-by" date. I've resold it four more times to different parenting markets since it first appeared. I also submitted and sold it to a parenting anthology. That makes six checks (so far) for one piece—not bad.

In the preceding three chapters, you've seen 12 examples of different articles and how to research and write them. You now have the basics you need to be able to do the same thing. When in doubt, always keep your readers (and your editor) and their interests and needs in mind. If you have a question during the researching and writing process, don't be afraid to talk to your editor about it. After all, she is person you're trying to please.

CHAPTER 10:
Build your Freelance Arsenal with the 10 Essential Templates

In a perfect world, you'd have all the time you want to write. In the real world, you're limited by the number of hours, or even minutes, you can spare for your work every day. Working efficiently will help you produce more writing regardless of how much time you can devote to your current project.

When you start out as a writer, *everything* takes longer than it will in the future. Keep this in mind if you struggle with writing queries or conducting research. As you gain experience, you'll naturally become more efficient, but let's focus on some other ways to make the most of your writing time.

There are endless ways to work more productively, but the first (and arguably most important) is to **protect your writing time**. If you've planned to spend two hours on Tuesday morning or Thursday evening working on queries, don't fritter that time away on Facebook! If you struggle with staying focused, use one of my tricks—set a timer for a certain amount of time (say, 30, 40, or 50 minutes), and force yourself to stay on task until the timer goes off. (Shut down your email program so you won't be distracted by incoming email, and ignore the phone, too. If you have family at home—especially small children—let them know that you're working and are not to be disturbed, unless there's "blood or broken bones," as one of my writer friends says.)

Second, look for ways to **get more from your writing time**. That's where templates come in. In the preceding chapters, you've seen some examples of the kinds of templates I use, but this chapter includes the ten you'll need the most as someone writing for money.

Feel free to base your own templates on mine, or simply use them as inspiration for your own. Once you have a template that you feel comfortable with, use it as the basis for your other queries, follow-up letters, etc. This simple step will save you tons of time and make you more productive.

The Top 10 Templates

There is no one "right" way to write an LOI, invoice, or thank-you note. However, you'll find that having a template as a guide speeds up the process, freeing up time for you get on with the business of freelancing. The following templates include: the query letter; the letter of introduction ("LOI"); the cover letter; the follow-up letter; the letter of agreement; the simple contract;

the invoice; the invoice follow-up; the pay-or-die letter; the interview contact email; and the thank-you note.

Each template includes a brief explanation of when it's used, the template itself, and my comments about the way it's written in brackets. Remember that these are designed to use as examples; feel free to "tweak" them to fit your personal voice and style. If they sound *exactly* like Kelly James-Enger wrote them, you probably need to rework them a bit.

The Query Letter to magazines

After 15 years of freelancing, I've written at least 1,200 query letters, or queries, and critiqued more than 1,000 for other writers. As a result, I know what works.

You read about query letters in chapter three, but let's review. The query letter, or query, is an essential tool for any freelancer who writes for print and online markets, but it needn't be complicated. I use a simple, four-section query for nearly all of mine that includes the following parts:

(1) The **lead**. Here I catch the editor's attention, usually with a recent study or other time peg, a startling (or at least interesting) statistic, or an anecdote.

(2) The **"why-write it"** section. Here I make the case for the piece, providing more details and basically explaining why readers will be interested in the story.

(3) The **"nuts-and-bolts"** section. Here I explain how I'll approach the story, suggesting word count, possible sources, and format (i.e. will the piece include a sidebar, or a quiz?). I also like to include a working title, and I always suggest the section of the publication the piece belongs in to let the editor know I've read her magazine.

(4) The **ISG**, or **"I'm-so-great"** section. Here I demonstrate that I'm uniquely qualified to write the piece and highlight my relevant background and experience.

Pretty simple, right? Here's a query template, with my comments in brackets.

Dear Pam:

It's a common conundrum. You've actually stuck to a regular workout routine, but you're still not seeing results. While "lack of time" is the number one excuse for not exercising, what's even more frustrating is making the time to hit the gym—and seeing no change in your body. What is the deal? [Here's my lead. It's not bad, but I could have cited a recent study to back up my "number one excuse" for not exercising. However, this lead is aimed at the readers of *Oxygen*--they're women who are serious about their workout regimes and their physiques.]

The culprit may be multifaceted. Driven by a desire to burn calories and get ripped, women commonly overlook (or deny) the importance of refueling their muscles with glycogen by consuming carbs (and protein, too) within the "magic window" that closes 45 minutes after intense exercise. Without adequate refueling, your regular routine may leave your muscles chronically depleted, which affects your energy level, motivation, and workout quality. [My "why-write-it" section is pretty good. Note the amount of research I've done here--yet again, I could have cited a recent study to strengthen the query.]

"Dumb Fitness Mistakes Even Smart Women Make" will examine some of the most common mistakes, how they impact (or prevent) desired results, and most important, how to overcome them. I plan to interview experts such as Tom Holland, MS/CSCS sports performance coach, and author of *The Truth about How to Get in Shape*, and Nancy Clark, RD, author of *The Sports Nutrition Guidebook, Fourth Edition*, for this story. While I estimate 1200 words for this story, that's flexible depending on your needs. [My nuts-and-bolts section is pretty good, too. Note I've told her the types of experts I plan to interview and provided a working title and word count. She can assign something different, but this gives her an idea of how I plan to approach the piece.]

Interested in this informative piece as a cover-lined fitness feature? [A "cover line" the headline that appears on a magazine's cover or Website's home page.] I've been a fulltime freelancer for more than a decade; my work has also appeared in magazines including *Redbook, Self, Health, Continental, Fitness, Woman's Day*, and *Shape*. I'm also an ACE-certified personal trainer, which will help bring a unique perspective to this piece. [My ISG is strong, and includes the fact that I'm a personal trainer. Even if I had no clips yet, that fact and a strong query would give me a good chance of getting my foot in the door.]

Please let me know if you have any questions about this pitch, and thank you for your time. [Standard close.]

Sincerely,
Kelly James-Enger

The Letter of Introduction

The query is the most popular way to pitch a magazine editor you want to work for. But there's another way to get your foot in the door with editors—by sending a letter of introduction, or LOI.

LOIs offer another method of snagging assignments from a variety of publications. I've used LOIs to break in with trade magazines, custom publishers, corporations, and book packagers, so I can tell you they work.

It's true that most consumer magazine editors want to receive queries from freelancers, especially those who are new to them. But many editors at custom publications and trade magazines *prefer* LOIs to queries. These editors already know what they're going to assign and they need writers who can handle their subject matter. Rather than using your letter to describe one story idea and how you'll approach it, an LOI gives you more space to describe your unique qualifications to report and write for the market.

If you do more than one type of writing work, I suggest you develop more than one LOI template. (For example, I have an LOI I use for possible ghostwriting projects, another for possible speaking gigs, and others for general freelancing work. Each highlights a different area of my expertise and experience.)

In some instances, you'll know something about the market or client you're pitching, and you can customize your LOI to reflect that fact. But what about when you're pitching "blind" and have no info about the market? Then highlight your qualifications that are likely to make you stand out from the pack.

Here's an LOI I sent to a post on craigslist seeking freelancers to write about specific health conditions:

Dear Sir or Madam:

I'm replying to your post on craigslist.org seeking freelancers for publications about MS, diabetes, cardiovascular disease, and obesity. I think I'm a perfect fit—in fact, I've written extensively about all of these conditions with the exception of MS. [This is a fairly simple introduction that hopefully demonstrates I'm just the writer the editor is looking for.]

I've been a fulltime freelancer for the last decade, and I specialize in health, fitness, nutrition, and wellness articles. More than 700 of my articles have appeared in 50 national magazines including *Redbook, Self, Health, Family Circle, Woman's Day, Continental, Fitness,* and *Shape.* I'm also the coauthor of *Small Changes, Big Results: A 12-Week Action Plan to a Better Life* (with Ellie Krieger, R.D./Random House, 2005), a nutrition/fitness/wellness book. [Here, I provide a brief bio, highlighting my health writing background. If I was contacting, say, a bridal publication, I'd play up my bridal writing experience. My point? Your LOI should emphasize whatever qualifications are relevant to this particular project you're pursuing.]

I've interviewed hundreds of health, fitness, and nutrition experts over the years and am a tireless researcher; also, as a self-admitted "type A", I *never* miss a deadline. I'm also an ACE-certified personal trainer, and speak and consult about subjects ranging from time management to goal-setting to getting (and staying) fit. I enjoy helping people make positive changes in their lives through my work as an author, journalist, and speaker. [Here I'm giving a little more detail about my background, including my research experience, which is relevant to this kind of work. I mention that I'm a personal trainer because that fact may help set me apart from the other freelancers pursuing this position. If I were sending an LOI going after, say, a ghostwriting position for a law firm, I'd mention that I was a lawyer in my former life. Get the idea?]

I'll be happy to send some clips via regular mail if you're interested. Please let me know if you have any questions about my background or experience; I look forward to hearing from you soon. [I'm willing to send clips, but I want the editor to request them. No sense in sending them unless he or she is interested in my work.]

Thanks for your time and consideration, and have a great day! [Standard closing language.]

Sincerely,
Kelly James-Enger

The Follow-Up Letter

The follow-up letter is one of the simplest to write, yet it's often overlooked. In fact, failing to follow up on a query or submission is a common freelance mistake. If you don't hear back from an editor, *always* send a follow-up letter.

Simply sending one demonstrates you're professional and taking your writing seriously. It increases not only the chance of a response, but of an assignment as well. (Hey, the editor may have overlooked or missed your query, or been meaning to get to it...your follow-up letter may make the difference.)

Wondering when to follow up? That depends on the publication's guidelines. If it says that it typically responds in six to eight weeks, I follow up in (you guessed it) six to eight weeks. If I've written for a market before, I follow up in two to three weeks. If the market is new to me and doesn't specify a typical response time, I usually follow up in about four to six weeks.

A follow-up need only include a few sentences. Here's a simple template for you to use:

Dear John:

Hope you're doing well. I'm writing to follow up on a query I sent you (working title, "Foot Form and Function") four weeks ago; I've dropped it below for your convenience. [Remind the editor which pitch you're following up on, and include it in your follow-up (in the body of the email, not as an attachment) to make it easy for him. If the editor you're pitching prefers to receive queries by snail mail, follow up by snail mail, and include a copy of the original query.]

Would you let me know at your earliest opportunity if you're interested in this story for *Chicago Athlete?* If I don't hear from you within two weeks, I'll assume you're not interested in the idea at this time and may market it elsewhere. [Here's the bonus of following up--you put the onus on the *editor* to get back to *you.* If she wants the piece, great! If not, I'm not going to sit around for months hoping for a response--I'm moving on, baby. I've found that I almost always get a response when I take the time to follow up. And note that the time you give a market to respond is up to you. You can give a market more time to respond--say three to four weeks--if you like. The idea is to give the editor a deadline to get back to you—otherwise, you move on and submit it to another market.]

Kelly James-Enger

Thank you very much for your time; I look forward to hearing from you [Standard closing line.]

Very truly yours,
Kelly James-Enger

The Cover Letter

Typically as a freelancer, you'll send a query or LOI to introduce yourself. However, to submit an essay or a humorous piece, you typically send the entire essay along with a cover letter. Then the editor decides whether she wants to purchase it.

Your goal with the cover letter is to entice your editor to read your essay. Introduce your piece and pique her interest with your cover letter to increase your chance of selling the piece to her.

Here's an example of a compelling cover letter:

Dear Tamara:

You may already be aware that November is National Adoption Month. According to the U.S. Census, there are 1.6 million adopted children under the age of 18 in this country, and 4 percent of all households contain adopted children. That makes it likely that someone close to you—a friend, a family member, a neighbor, or a coworker—has been touched by adoption. [This lead shows that the subject matter of the essay—adoption—is likely to impact many of her readers' lives.]

Until recently, adoptions were almost always "closed," meaning that records were sealed and birth and adoptive parents didn't know each others' identities, let alone have contact with each other. Today, however, more adoptive parents have "open" adoptions, where they maintain a relationship with their child's birth parents. [Here I provide a little more detail about the subject of the essay, which will hopefully catch her interest.]

My enclosed essay, "Keeping an Open Heart," explains this unique relationship and how it impacts me as a mom (through adoption) to my two-year-old son. I hope you'll find it appropriate for the "Reader Essay" slot of an upcoming issue (perhaps in November?) of *Chicago Parent*. [Here I finally introduce the essay, and tell her where I think it belongs. Hopefully she'll agree.]

Tamara, let me know if you have any questions about this essay, and have a great day! Thanks for your time and consideration. [Fairly typical closing language.]

All my best,
Kelly

The Letter of Agreement

When you freelance for many publications, your editor will send you a contract to sign setting out the terms of your agreement. But what about when you take an assignment for a market that doesn't have a standard contract? Then you'll want to draft your own contract. I gave you an example of a simple contract in chapter 5, but you can also use a letter of agreement to serve the same purpose.

It's not as complicated as you might think. To create an enforceable agreement, you must include the following:

The **date**;
A **statement/description of the work** you're performing;
The **deadline** for the work;
A description of the **rights** being purchased (for example, "all rights" or "reprint rights");
The amount of **money** you're being paid, and when; and
The **name**/identity of your client.

I like to keep my letters of agreement simple. Here's an example of one I used when an editor hired me to "tweak," or rework, a reprint to better fit her audience.

October 21, 2009

Dear Kathleen:

Thanks for getting in touch; I'm looking forward to working with you! I'm writing to confirm our discussion of today where we agreed that I'll rework my resolutions piece for you by October 31, 2009. I'll provide a 1,200-word article aimed at an audience of both men and women, and you'll pay me $200 for one-time reprint rights to the story. [I've set out what I've agreed to do for her, including my pay and the deadline.]

Please confirm this agreement by replying to this email, and I'll get to work! Thank you very much and I'll talk to you soon. [Basic closing language.]

Sincerely,
Kelly James-Enger

See how simple a letter of agreement is? I often use them with new clients. If you want a signature from your client (which may make the agreement easier to enforce should you encounter payment problems), you can email your client and ask him to print, sign, and return the contract to you, or send the letter of agreement by mail and ask that it be signed and returned.

The Invoice

In some cases, when you submit an article or completed assignment to an editor, she'll arrange for you to be paid. Most of the time, however, you must submit an invoice. For that, you need a simple template that includes a date, invoice number (which makes it easier for the Accounts Payable department to track it), amount, and statement of what rights are being purchased/what you're invoicing for. You may also need to include your social security or tax ID number on the invoice; ask your client if this is necessary. (Keep in mind that most clients will have you fill out a W-9 form when you turn in your first assignment, so they'll already have your social security number.)

Easy, right? Here's one you can use as a template:

July 17, 2007

Beth Smith, Editor in Chief
Sports and Fitness Magazine

Re: INVOICE #643 [Always include an invoice number!]

Dear Beth:

Please let this email serve as my invoice for $500 for first North American serial rights and nonexclusive electronic rights to "Walk Away the Weight" per written contract of June 15, 2007. My mailing address is below. [Simple, to-the-point language. If you have a written agreement, reference it. Otherwise, describe the work you're invoicing for.]

Thank you very much! I hope we'll have the chance to work together again soon. [It never hurts to be nice.]

Best,
Kelly James-Enger
[Mailing address and contact information]

When you send an invoice (or when a story is accepted and your editor puts payment through), make a note of it on your calendar. Then if you haven't been paid in four to six weeks, follow up on the outstanding invoice. Staying on top of your "accounts receivable" is part of running your freelance business.

The Invoice Follow-Up

What happens when you don't get paid in a timely manner? If you're me, you get annoyed, angry, frustrated, you name it. That's normal. But as a working writer, you need to stay on top of your invoices. If you haven't been paid, follow up on your missing money with an email like the following:

September 4, 2007

Beth Smith, Editor in Chief
Sports and Fitness Magazine

Re: INVOICE #643 [Always include an invoice number!]

Dear Beth:

I hope you're doing well, first off. I'm writing to follow up on the outstanding invoice for my piece, "Walk Away the Weight." I emailed the invoice on July 17, but still haven't received payment. Would you let me know when I can expect to receive my check for this story? Or if there is someone else I should follow up with in the accounts payable department, let me know and I'll contact him or her. [I let the editor know what I've done so far to get paid.]

Thank you so much for your help with this. I look forward to working with you again. [I strive for a professional but friendly tone with this type of letter. There's a good chance that my editor had nothing to do with me not getting paid—but at the same time, she's probably in the best position to help me get paid. So I ask for her cooperation. This letter almost always works.]

Best,
Kelly James-Enger
[Mailing address and contact information]

The Pay-or-Die Letter

Let's say your polite, professional follow-up doesn't result in getting paid. Now what?

In 16 years of freelancing I've only dealt with slow-pay or "no-pay" clients about a dozen times. That's fortunate, but it doesn't make it any less annoying when a client fails to pay you. Usually sending an invoice, and staying on top of it, is all you have to do to get paid.

But when a client doesn't pay you in a reasonable time frame, check the terms of your contract—more publishers are opting for longer payment cycles—and make it your goal to collect what you're owed. Yes, you can call and send emails, but at a certain point, you need a formal demand for payment, or what I call a "pay-or-die" letter.

The point of the pay-or-die letter is to get paid—without burning your bridges. (Hey, you never know where an editor may end up. Even if I know I don't want to work for a particular market again, I try to terminate the relationship without getting nasty.)

A pay-or-die letter includes the terms of your assignment (referring to your written contract if you have one), demonstrates that you have satisfied your obligations, describes the attempts you've taken to get paid, and asks for immediate payment. I've found that threatening to turn the matter over to my attorney usually provokes payment.

To speed up the process, find out who actually cuts the checks and pursue that person for payment. You can certainly enlist your editor's help, but I've found that going to the person who holds the purse strings gets me paid more quickly.

Here's a simple pay-or-die letter you can tweak to fit your needs. In this instance, Mr. Nopay (yes, that's a made-up name) is the owner of a small publishing company who owes me for an article. I send a letter like this by regular mail, return receipt requested, so I know the recipient got it okay.

Dear Mr. Nopay:

I'm writing to formally request payment for the article I turned in three months ago. Per the terms of my contract, I am to be paid upon acceptance, and my editor, Marie Underling, accepted the article on February 28, 2007. It is now June 2, 2007, and I still haven't been paid. [Simple, clear language that sets out the problem, sticking to the facts.]

I have complied with all of the terms of my agreement and have emailed Ms. Underling and spoken with her by phone several times regarding this matter. At her suggestion, I have contacted the Accounts Payable department of your magazine on three occasions. Each time I have been assured that I will be paid "immediately" but still have not received my check. [Again, I'm explaining what has happened without specifically placing blame. But I want Mr. Nopay to know what steps I have taken to get paid, and that they have all failed.]

I ask that you immediately issue me a check for **$1,200.00**, the amount I'm owed per the terms of our written contract dated January 7, 2007. If I do not receive full payment within **five business days**, I'll turn the matter over to my attorney. [Here's the heart of the matter. I'm telling him what he needs to do—or else. Will I turn this over to my attorney? It depends on the amount owed. But I've found that often a letter threatening legal action gets me my money. And that's what I want.]

Thank you for your prompt attention to this matter. I look forward to hearing from you and receiving my check soon. [See, you can be persistent, professional, and polite, even with a pay-or-die letter.]

Very truly yours,
Kelly James-Enger

The Interview Contact Note

As a freelancer who writes nonfiction, you'll be contacting sources—both experts and "real people" for anecdotes—for many of the articles you write. While I prefer to conduct interviews by telephone (I feel it makes for more compelling quotes and it's easier for my subject to talk instead of having to write up his or her answers to my questions), but I often *schedule* the interview via email.

For this kind of note, you want to explain who you are, why you're getting in touch, what you're looking for in terms of the interview, and ask the person to respond to your request.

Here's a template to use:

Dear Dr. Domar: [Keep it formal if you haven't met this person before; I use Mr., Ms., or Dr., depending on the person's title.]

I'm a freelance writer who's working on an article about ways to better manage stress for *Chicago Parent*, a regional parenting magazine. I'm contacting you because I'm familiar with your work at the Domar Center for Mind-Body Health, and I think you'd make an excellent source for this piece. [I've introduced myself, told her how I know about her, and explained what I want from her. If I got her name from someone else, I'd mention that in my opening paragraph.]

Are you available in the next three days to do a brief (10-15 minutes, max) interview by telephone? I'm happy to work around your schedule, or if you prefer, I can send you questions via email. [So, here's what I want—an interview with her in the next three days. I'd also told her how long I need, and given her the option of doing the interview by email. I'm trying to demonstrate that I respect her time and want to make it easy for her to speak with me.]

Please let me know at your earliest convenience if you're interested and available, and I'll be back in touch. Thank you so much for your time, and for considering this request. [This is my standard closing language. Manners make a difference!]

Sincerely,
Kelly James-Enger
[contact info]

The Thank-You Note

Surprised by this template? You shouldn't be. The thank-you note should be part of every freelancer's arsenal. I send a personal thank-you to sources I interview, to people who refer clients to me, and to others who go "above and beyond" for me. And while a thank-you doesn't take that much effort, it's likely to be remembered by your recipient.

Here's an example of one I'd send after an interview:

Dear Alice,

Thank you so much for speaking with me this morning about ways for busy parents to better manage stress. You gave me some great quotes and background for this article for *Chicago Parent*, and I really appreciate your time and help. I'll be in touch with any follow-up questions or to let you know when the piece runs. [Simple but genuine expression of thanks. I send these notes via snail mail. Yes, it's more expensive, but I think the extra effort makes them stand out even more.]

Thanks again and have a great day!

Sincerely,
Kelly James-Enger

And here's an example of a note I sent to an expert who had referred a new client to me:

Dear Brad:

I just wanted to say thanks for passing my name along to Jonathan Goodman; I really appreciate it! He's hired me, and I'm excited about working with him on his book project. Thanks again for thinking of me, and have a great week! [I've used Brad as a source in the past—he's a nationally known personal trainer and author—but I still take the time to thank him with a personal note.]

All my best,
Kelly

I'll even send a thank-you via email to an editor I'm working with, saying something like:

Dear Sarah:

Thanks for sending me the galleys of the new "Freelance Success" column. It looks great, and your edits tightened the piece and made it stronger. I appreciate your hard work!

Have a great day,
Kelly

Get the idea? A thank-you note does more than express your appreciation; it makes you more memorable, helps you stand out from the freelance pack, and helps you create relationships with people. In my mind, that makes them significant—and one of the ten templates that you should have in your freelance arsenal.

CHAPTER 11
When the Worst Happens: 15 Freelance Crises and How to Handle Them

So far, I think you've gotten a pretty good overview of how to start writing for money. But sometimes things go wrong, and bad things happen to even the best writers. So this chapter addresses 15 fairly common freelance crises, and how to respond if they happen.

Freelance crisis: you've had no response from an editor.

As in, you've queried a market and all you hear is crickets. Now what?

First, if you're talking about a query, have you sent a follow-up? When you followed up, did you give your editor a deadline? If she hasn't responded, then move on to the next market.

If you're talking about turning in an article, and you haven't had a response for several weeks, then you need to be proactive. Send an email to your editor, attaching the story again, and say something like, "Hi, Sue. I'm just writing to follow up on the story I turned in three weeks ago. Could you let me know if you have any questions about the piece? Thanks very much for your time."

You're not being a pest—with some editors, you have to stay on top of them to make sure they've received your piece and that you get paid for it. If it's a new market for you, make sure you know whether you need to submit an invoice or not to get paid.

Freelance crisis: you can't find the source you need.

In chapter 7, you learned how to find expert sources. If you've tried all of those techniques, you should be able to locate an appropriate expert. If for some reason no one will agree to talk to you for the article, and you've reached out to several (at least four or five), let your editor know that you're having trouble locating the person you need and ask for her input.

I will say, though, that I have *never* been unable to find appropriate experts for every piece I've written. What's trickier, and what I sometimes dread, is finding those real people to include as anecdotes. Occasionally I'll know someone who fits the bill from the outset, like when I interviewed a guy I know from my gym about his weight lifting and nutrition program for an article for a men's fitness magazine. Sometimes, though, you have to go to great lengths to find who you need, whether you're looking for a parent of twins who home-schools, a millionaire who rents a one-bedroom apartment, or a married couple who "swing."

As I said earlier, I use social media (primarily Facebook and Twitter) to locate anecdotal sources. But that's usually my last resort. I'll try to find people using sites like HARO and by reaching out to relevant organizations for leads. So, for example, when I needed to interview a mother who was diagnosed with heart disease at a relatively young age, I emailed the American Heart Association. The public affairs person had the name and contact info of an excellent source for me in less than 48 hours. Online bulletin boards and communities are also possibilities for locating sources.

If you still can't locate a critical source, or if the person you need won't speak with you, tell your editor and see what she suggests. Just don't wait until the last minute to drop this on her. And make sure you tell her all of the legwork you've done already. She should be able to suggest an alternative or come up with a different angle or approach to the story.

Freelance crisis: the editor stole your idea!

I get asked about editors stealing ideas a lot. Yet this doesn't happen as often as you might expect. It's not uncommon for writers to pitch similar ideas at the same time—we're following the same trends, after all. And think about how many "New Year's resolutions" stories get pitched to health, fitness, men's and women's magazines every year. I'd wager it's in the hundreds if not thousands. My point? Pitching an idea that later shows up in the market under another writer's name doesn't mean the editor stole it. She may have already had something similar in the works because another writer beat you to it.

However. Let's say you've pitched a very specific idea—a profile on a particular person, or a piece reporting on a research breakthrough that hasn't been publicized. You never heard back from the editor, or he rejects it, and then you see "your" story a few weeks or months later in your target publication. In that case, did the editor take your idea? Well, maybe, especially if you're a new writer. But the best way to prevent this from happening is always keep that uniquely qualified concept idea in mind when querying a market, and to start out pitching shorter pieces. That will help convince an editor to give you a chance.

Freelance crisis: you made a mistake.

This happens to every writer, including me. I had a source with a complicated last name, and I managed to spell his name three different ways in one article. I was sloppy in my proofreading (confession: I don't think I proofed the piece, period), and my editor sent me an email, asking me to double-check the spelling of his name. I was embarrassed, especially because I'd written for her before.

I'll tell you the truth. I did a half-assed job on this story, rushed the process, and it showed. Let me tell you, I apologized big-time, and promised her it would *never* happen again. I was fortunate in that she continued to work with me, but that sloppiness could have easily lost me a client.

Make sure you take the time to spell out sources' names and that you double-check statistics and other facts as you're writing the story. Then I suggest you print the piece out and read it out loud to catch as many imperfections as you can. When a mistake eventually squeaks through, don't lose your mind. Admit it and apologize to the editor—and make sure it never happens again. Then move on. Obsessing over it won't get you anywhere.

Freelance crisis: you've received the assignment. But you don't know what it pays.

This happened to a friend of mine. She got an assignment from a market but the editor didn't tell her how much she was paying her. To me, it was obvious—email the editor and ask!

"I'm embarrassed," she admitted. "It makes me look clueless."

"Or it makes the editor looks clueless," I pointed out. "Email her and gently point out that she forgot one of the specs of the assignment. I'm sure it was an oversight." It was, and the editor replied to her immediately with the rate. If you're in this situation, make sure you double-check your pay before you proceed with an assignment. You don't want to write an article to find out you're being paid a pittance, or for "the exposure."

Freelance crisis: you didn't set aside money for taxes.

The good news? You made more money than you expected this year. The bad news? You didn't set any aside to pay your taxes. And you're broke.

First, if this is you, apply for an extension with the IRS to give yourself time to collect the money you need to pay. And in the future, I suggest you set a certain amount—say, 15 or 20 percent—aside so that you don't run into this problem in the future. And remember to treat your writing like a business, so you can deduct your writing-related expenses and lower your overall tax liability.

Freelance crisis: you hate the edited version of your story.

You wrote a fantastic article, then your editor went and slashed it to pieces. Now it doesn't even sound like you. You're annoyed, maybe even angry.

My advice? Let it go. Your editor's job is to take your words and make them work for her readers. That's what she gets paid for. If the edit is so atrocious you can't breathe, yeah, you can ask to have your name taken off the story if you see the galleys [the final version of the story before it goes to print] before the story runs. (Some publications send writers galleys, but the majority of them do not.) Otherwise, decide whether you want to continue to work with the heavy-penned editor and move on. ("Move on" isn't bad advice for handling many freelance crises, in fact!)

Freelance crisis: your story got killed.

Remember when we talked about kill fees in chapter 5? They're fine in theory—until it's *your* story that is the one getting killed. Then it feels really personal. And icky.

Sometimes stories are killed because the writer didn't deliver what the assignment entailed. You had a chance and you blew it. In other cases, a story gets killed because an editor has changed his mind about what he's going to run—or his boss has changed his mind. Regardless, your story's been axed.

If you feel that you met the specs of your assignment, push for full payment from your editor. It's worth a polite email reminding him that you met the terms of your agreement, and asking to be paid in full. Chances are that you're still collecting nothing more than a kill fee, but it doesn't hurt to try.

Next step, consider alternative markets for your killed piece. Rework your initial query, or write one if the editor came to you with the idea, and pitch that sucker somewhere else. You don't have to reveal that you've written a story on the subject already—when a piece is killed, all rights revert back to you. If you can sell the piece as written, great. Otherwise, don't be afraid to harvest your killed story for quotes, anecdotes, even whole paragraphs. No one will know the difference and your job after having a story killed to find another market you can sell it to.

Freelance crisis: you can't make your deadline.

For whatever reason—a sick kid, a sick cat, circumstances outside your control—you can't make your deadline. Or maybe you screwed up and didn't give yourself enough time to research and write the story, and now you're stuck.

Suck it up. You blew it, so don't try to ignore the assignment or hope your editor won't notice when deadline day goes by and your story is AWOL. Let your editor know that you won't make your deadline as soon as you know it, apologize, and ask her for a few more days. Then work your butt off to get that story done and meet your new deadline. Turn in a solid story and she'll be willing to overlook the fact it wasn't on time. And in the future, give yourself more time to complete assignments, or turn down stories you know you won't be able to finish in time.

Freelance crisis: your editor wants you to rewrite the story.

This isn't a crisis, first off. This is part of writing for money. Ask your editor why the piece isn't working for her. Some editors will give you very detailed notes, which makes your job easier. Others will say something like, "I don't know … but it's not working for me … I'm not sure why…" which makes your job, well, more challenging. If you get edit notes via email, read through them and make sure you know what you need to do to make your editor happy. If you have any questions, clarify via email or ask to speak to your editor by phone.

And double-check when your editor needs the piece back by. I've found that editors like revisions turned around as quickly as possible, so your willingness to do the same will help endear you to them.

As a new writer, you're likely to get revision requests. That's normal, especially when you're writing for a market that's new to you. I've had to revise several stories more than once—one piece, four times before it met with my editor's approval. Was I happy about all the extra work? Nope—but I was relieved to have that sucker off of my desk, and finally get paid for it!

Freelance crisis: you've done all the research. But you're paralyzed by the thought of writing the article.

This happens to every freelancer. If you're stuck, I suggest you read through your query again (if you have one), your research, and your transcripts. What jumps out at you? Pull some quotes that "pop," start your lead, or make a list of the points you know you want to include in the piece. Just do something. Even if you churn out what Anne Lamott calls a "shitty first draft," you can edit it afterwards.

Stuck on a word or have to double-check something while you're writing your first draft? Don't get bogged down. Use my "TK" trick instead. "TK" is an editing term that means "to come." I use TK as a placeholder and reminder to double-check the word, fact, or missing information later on, and keep on writing until I have my first draft in the can. Then I address any TKs during my second or third draft. That strategy alone makes me a much faster, more efficient writer.

Freelance crisis: you received the contract for your first article for a market, and you don't want to sign it.

What's the problem with the contract? Is it for "all rights" when you only wanted to sell first rights? Or does it have a nasty indemnification provision? Is the contract a deal-breaker for you?

If it is, try to get your editor to change it. If he can't, or won't, it's now up to you to decide whether you'll accept it or not. I've signed contracts I wasn't thrilled about when I couldn't get certain language changed and I needed the work and the money. I've turned down contracts, too, but almost always because the money offered for the piece wasn't enough. If the money's fair, I'll sign a contract that is far from writer-friendly. To me, that's part of writing for money.

Freelance crisis: you haven't been paid for your story.

This will happen to you at some point. Stay on top of any outstanding invoices, and send your editor a note if you are waiting on a check six to eight weeks after you turn the story in. (If you're writing for a market that pays on publication, give the market four weeks after the story first runs.) And if you still haven't been paid, follow the steps (and feel free to use the templates) in chapter 10.

In nearly 16 years of freelancing, I've only been stiffed a handful of times. Usually persistence will get you paid, so don't give up until you collect that check!

Freelance crisis: you've been published, and now everyone wants you to help them write for money too.

That's not a crisis! Tell them to buy this book! And if they read the whole thing and still have questions, point them to my blog, below.

Freelance crisis: You've got a question that isn't answered in this book.

No problem. Check out my blog (http://dollarsanddeadlines.blogspot.com) first—I've got hundreds of posts addressing common freelancing issues. Didn't turn up the answer? Then shoot me an email at dollarsanddeadlines@gmail.com and I'll get back to you in a day or two. Just keep your email and your question concise, please, and I'll be happy to respond.

CHAPTER 12
What's Next? Expanding your Writing Career

You're no longer a newbie. You've followed the advice in this book. You've researched markets and pitched ideas. You've been rejected—and survived. Better yet, you've received assignments. You've conducted interviews with utter strangers, yet managed to get solid information and hopefully compelling quotes out of them. You've written articles. Maybe you've rewritten them. You've seen your byline in print and/or pixels. And you've been paid.

You have **written for money**! Go you!

At some point, though, you may think, um, okay … so what's next? That's up to you.

One of the aspects of freelancing I love—and many others do as well—is that I work for myself. My success, or failure, is in my own hands.

That fact can present a problem, though. As a freelancer, you don't have a boss or supervisor you can rely on for an annual review. You don't have anyone who will alert you to new opportunities, suggest that you acquire new skills, or help you develop a successful career path. It's all up to you, once again!

But I'm going to give you some advice. If you've reached the point where you're writing articles regularly, you may want to start working more efficiently, making more money, or both. Let's talk about ways to do both.

Narrow your Focus

As a new writer, you may be pitching any and every idea you can come up. That's what I did, too. But I've found that it's inefficient to be a generalist. If you want to make more money and be more efficient, I suggest you specialize.

Yet freelancers often resist the idea of limiting themselves to a subject area or two. After all, we're often attracted to freelancing because of the freedom it gives us. We can write about anything we want! The idea of being told what we can write, or can't, makes us itchy, right?

It shouldn't. I know hundreds of successful freelancers. And I'd say that about 90 percent of them specialize. They're not trying to write about anything and everything--they're choosing to limit what they write about for these six reasons:

1. Deeper background. Much of your time as a freelancer is devoted to researching articles. Specializing lets you develop a knowledge base in a particular area, which means you spend less time researching and more time actually writing. If you write about nutrition, for example, you probably already know how many grams of protein an egg has, or why coconut oil is a hot topic right now. If you cover parenting, you're familiar with terms like "family bed," "nipple confusion," and "attachment parenting."

2. Higher assignment rate. You're an editor who gets two pitches on the subject of growing your own herbs. One is from a generalist; one is from a writer who specializes in cooking and food. If the queries are of similar quality, the editor's more likely to choose the specialist because of the perceived value that the specialist knows more--and she probably does.

3. More money. That perceived value I just mentioned? Editors will pay you more when you have experience covering a subject. I've used the fact that I'm a health/wellness writer to ask for, and get, higher per-word rates for stories.

4. Memorable identity. You want your editors to remember you, and think of you for assignments. I just had an editor contact me today asking if I have any articles on breast cancer, because she knows I cover health. Other editors contact me specifically because they have fitness-related stories to assign and know that I develop and write workout pieces.

5. Deeper inventory. Most writers don't bother trying to sell reprint rights to their stories because the publications that purchase them don't pay much for reprints. Well, when you specialize, you have a whole trove of stories to offer, which makes you more likely to sell multiple reprints--and again, develop an identity that editors will remember. [See below section.]

6. Potential platform. Want to write a book or e-book in the future? Then you'll need a platform, or an ability to sell the book to readers. For many writers, including me, specializing is the first step to developing a platform.

Still waffling? Remember, specializing doesn't *prevent* you from writing about anything you want to. You still have that option. (Even I venture out of my health/fitness/nutrition pigeonhole occasionally to tackle new subjects.) Specializing *does* mean that you focus on your unique strengths and background, whether you're a new writer or a more seasoned one. Specializing helps you market more efficiently. It can help you develop a name for yourself. It can help you sell more of your work, and be paid more for that work. And over time, it can transform a so-so freelance career into one that lets you reach your dreams and monetary goals.

Write Once, Sell Twice (or More)

Selling, or licensing reprint rights to the articles you've already written, is one of the easiest ways to make money. So it's not surprising that according to my 2012 survey of writers, 18 percent of freelancers sell reprint rights to their work.

Keep in mind that you must retain rights to your work to be able to sell reprints. If you agree to an all-rights contract, you're left with nothing to sell, another reason to read those freelance contracts carefully. If a publication wants all rights, don't be afraid to ask if you can retain "nonexclusive reprint rights" to your work. Retaining those means that while the publisher can still do anything it wants with your work for no additional money, *you* are also free to offer reprint rights to markets that may not care that it's been published before.

No, you won't get rich selling reprints. Smaller, regional publications may pay between $25-$100/story while other markets may pay $150-250/story or more. Markets that are willing to purchase rights to stories don't pay as much as national consumer magazines, but that doesn't mean you shouldn't pursue them. After all, a reprint is basically "found" money.

To sell reprints, look for smaller, regional, or special interest magazines that have smaller budgets than their national counterparts. *Writer's Market* lists reprints, as do publications like the *Standard Periodical Directory*, which your local library should have on reserve. You'll find thousands of potential markets there, divided into categories. And don't forget to Google possible markets by searching for "magazine" and a particular subject or topic.

When you've found a potential market, send a quick email to see if it purchases reprint rights to stories that have been published before. (This information may also be included in its writers' guidelines.) Then send a brief LOI introducing yourself and include a list of the articles you have available for reprint, along with their word count, and ask if the editor is interested in purchasing rights to any of them.

If I get no response, I simply continue to update my story list with available work, and then contact the client again a few months later. After doing this for years, I know I have about a dozen reprint markets that purchase from me occasionally. No, I won't get rich selling reprints, but they comprise about 10 percent of my income each year, which makes them worthwhile.

Get More Regulars

I didn't set out as a freelancer trying to build relationships with editors and other clients. I just wanted clips, experience, and money—not necessarily in that order. But over time, I learned. And one thing I learned is that it's much easier (not to mention less stressful) and less time-consuming to work for a handful of editors on a regular basis than to do lots of "one-shots," where I write for a client or editor once and then move on.

So how do you do that? How do you make an editor or client a "regular"? It's not that complicated when you keep these seven tips in mind:

Pursue long-term markets. No more one-shots for me—I'm looking for markets I can write for multiple times. I'm selective in the markets I pitch. I look for those that I can have long-term relationships with—which usually translates into less time pitching and more work. Sounds obvious, but I've written for markets as varied as *The Lion* to *Accent on Living* to *Continental*—but all only once. On the other hand, I've written for other markets—like *Woman's Day, Complete Woman,* and *The Writer*—dozens of times over the years. Look for markets that buy a fair amount of freelance work, that cover subjects you write about, and that you feel fit your voice. That will help ensure long-term relationships.

Be generous when you can. Earlier this year, an editor asked me if I could add a quiz to a story I'd already turned in. I'd originally thought about doing a quiz but the story ran long, so I didn't include it. I briefly considered asking for more money; after all, she's asking for more work. Then I reconsidered. She's been giving me a lot of work lately, edits are minimal, and I like the story assignments I get. I emailed her back and told her I'd be happy to do it gratis and turned it in the next day. (No, I don't do that on a regular basis. I can't afford it. But I figure it's an investment in our relationship.)

Do what you say you'll do. I'm telling you, writers blow this all the time. Doing what you promised means more than meeting your deadline. It also means giving the editor what she asked for in terms of subject, slant, sources, and word count. It means turning in clean copy that's free of misspellings, factual errors, grammatical mistakes, and the like. If you can't do what you promised (say, you can't meet the deadline), tell your editor. Don't do what a writer I know did and simply "go rogue" and disappear for weeks. Needless to say, she never wrote for our mutual editor again!

Be low-maintenance. One of the nicest compliments I've ever had as a freelancer was when an editor told me I'm a "low-maintenance writer." I know what she meant. It's not just the quality of your wok that determines whether you'll get assignments. Other factors—like how quickly you respond to requests for revisions (which I know we all hate!), how diligent you are about coming up with story ideas, and even how pleasant you are—can all play a role as well.

Always have a back-pocket idea. When is an editor most disposed to give you an assignment? When she emails you to say "great job on this story," "I'm putting payment through," or some variation of the same. That's why I like to have an idea at the ready to pitch--I figure there's no better time to have her say "yes" again than when she's happy with a previous assignment. Don't let too much time lapse between pitches--ideally, have a new idea for an editor within two weeks of having her accept a piece.

Stay on their radar. I'm not my editors' only freelancer, and I know it. So I try to touch base with my regular clients every few months, even it's only a quick email. Sure, I let this slide when I'm busy, but an email that says something along the lines of "just checking in—I'm working on some new ideas for you, so let me know if you're looking for anything in particular" can often pay off with work. If I see a recent study, blog post, or news item I think will interest an editor, I'll email it just as an "FYI." No, my editors and clients aren't my buddies. (Okay, a few have become buddies, actually. But that kind of effort helps cement a relationship with someone I may never meet in person!)

Keep your bridges in place. Not all clients turn into long-term ones. That's just part of the business of freelancing. And there are editors I don't care to work with again. But they don't know who they are. They just know that I am incredibly busy when they call me…and after a few calls, they move on. In the meantime, I haven't burned any bridges—especially important as I never know where they may wind up. And who knows, I may work with them again one day…and I want to keep that option open.

Create an Online Presence

Remember in chapter 3 when I said you didn't need to worry about your social media presence? Well, once you've got some clips, I think it's worthwhile to create an online identity. A simple Website that gives your name and contact information and lets you showcase some of your work is all you need to get started. For simple but effective websites, take a look at Sam Greengard's (www.greengard.com); Susan Johnstons's (www.susan-johnston.com); Leslie Pepper's (http://www.lesliepepper.com/home/); and Gina Roberts-Grey's (http://ginaroberts-grey.com).

As far as social media goes, I consider LinkedIn and Twitter the best ways to connect with editors and other writers. LinkedIn is a kind of virtual resume and a professional way to present yourself to potential and current clients. I suggest you only "connect" on LinkedIn with people you know, know of, or have worked with. If there's an editor you're interested in working with, you can check to see whether one of your connections has worked with the editor before and use the "request an introduction" feature. If you get an invite to connect with someone you don't recognize, send them a message asking them to remind you how the two of you know each other. Then you can decide whether you want to connect or not.

If you're on Facebook, consider whether you want to connect with editors there. I'm friends with several of my editors on Facebook, and I know other writers who friend their regular editors, too. Remember, though, that many people like to keep their personal and professional lives separate, and may not be interested in connecting with you on Facebook. Whatever social media platform you use, be aware that anything you post online may be seen by anyone. Don't write or post anything that could hurt your chances with an editor or publication in the future.

I still believe that an online presence isn't a necessity for newbie writers. However, Google any fulltime freelancers and you'll find that he or she has, at the minimum, a Website. Many also have blogs, LinkedIn, and Twitter accounts. What you choose is up to you, but be sure that you're presenting a professional freelance persona through your social media accounts. You never know when an editor may come across your online presence, after all.

Grow in a New Direction

Finally, writing articles for print and online publications is a great way to launch a freelance career. But now that you have some experience under your belt, it may be time to move on—or at least expand the types of writing projects you do. Have you thought about ghostwriting? Making the jump from writing articles to writing books? Doing copywriting or other types of work for businesses?

At the beginning of this book, I suggested that you start thinking about the experience and knowledge you already had to prepare to pitch, sell, and write articles for money. Do the same thing now. What kinds of markets are you writing for? What subjects have you learned about? What do you want to know more about? What skills have you developed that you can use to tackle other kinds of writing projects?

The three most popular, and arguably easiest ways to expand your writing career are the following:

Editing

What it is: If you write, you also edit—at least your own work. Plenty of freelancers also provide editing services to a variety of clients. There are different types of editing—with developmental editing, you typically help the writer shape a project; substantive editing, where you work to improve a particular manuscript; or line editing, where you both edit and proofread the piece. If you're a good writer, you're probably a good editor, too, so it's not surprising that 46 percent of freelancers edit for pay as well.

What it pays: As a freelance editor, you set your own rates, which are usually per hour, per word, or per page. Experienced editors' rates vary, but typical rates range from $25-50/hour; $0.01-0.03/word; or $2-10/page.

Where to find markets/clients: Just as with ghostwriting (see below), you'll want to let everyone know that you're in the editing business. Check sites like FreelanceDaily.net, JournalismJobs.com, and CraigsList.org, and watch for ads from private companies and publishers, which often hire editors on a freelance basis.

How to break in: If you haven't done freelance editing before and you're unsure of your skills, consider asking a friend to do some editing for him or her so can you practice—and get an idea of how long the work tends to take you. Once you've got a couple of editing jobs under your belt, you can let people know that you're now doing freelance editing as well.

Writing for Businesses/Corporations

What it is: This is arguably one of the most lucrative types of markets for freelancers. Businesses both large and small hire writers to pen everything from brochures and ads to newsletters, Websites, and sales letters. Four in ten freelancers include this type of work in their mix.

What it pays: It depends on your experience. Seasoned copywriters charge $150/hour and up. Most freelancers, though, charge around $40-50/hour for business writing, gradually increasing their rates as they gain experience.

Where to find markets/clients: You may want to start locally, with the companies you're familiar with. Make a list of companies that are big enough that they may need a writer, and check sites like CraigsList.org for leads. Tell people in your community that you're a business writer, too; many of these projects are gained through word-of-mouth. Once you have your foot in the door with a particular company, make sure you ask for referrals. When you've done a good job for one company, your client is likely to refer to others—just not his or her biggest competitors.

How to break in: Create an LOI that describes not only your writing experience but highlights your background as well. For example, when I sent an LOI to The Pampered Chef, looking for freelance work, I mentioned that I had written about food and nutrition, and that I owned several Pampered Chef cooking tools. (Did I use them often? No…but you want to play up your strengths, and downplay any weaknesses.)

Follow up on your LOI, and ask if you can meet in person or send samples of your work. Many companies won't have a need for a writer when you contact them, but simply ask politely if you can keep in touch, say every six months or so. This helps keep you on their radar.

If you haven't done any kind of writing for businesses before, you may want to take on some volunteer projects to build up your portfolio. For example, I wrote brochures for organizations like my local chapter of Big Brothers/Big Sisters and web copy for my chamber of commerce so I had samples to show potential clients. They usually want you to have already done the kind of work they're hiring you to do, after all.

Ghostwriting

What it is: Ghostwriting is when you write something (typically books, articles, or blog posts) for a client whose name then appears on the finished product. As the "ghost," you get no formal recognition for your work but the market for ghostwriters is continuing to grow. (I've been ghosting and coauthoring for nearly a decade, and my most lucrative book projects so far have been those that I've written for others.)

Ghostwriting is unlike other writing work in that you have to be able capture your client's voice on the page, and to make your work sound, not like yourself, but like him. This means you must be able to set your ego aside (this isn't *your* work, after all—it's your clients) and keep your client's wants in your mind at all time. If you enjoy collaborating, though, it's a rewarding way to freelance for the one in six freelancers who chooses to do it.

What it pays: Typical ghostwriting projects pay a project fee, or a set amount for the work. While there are always clients offering to pay for a "share of the profits" (which could be zero!), I've found that the going rate for ghosted book proposals is in the $3,000-$10,000 range (depending on the length and complexity of the project). Pay for a complete ghostwritten book ranges in the $10,000-25,000 and up range. When it comes to articles, as the ghostwriter, you can set your own rates. I usually charge at least $1/word for ghostwritten articles and blog posts, and have found this rate is consistent with what other ghosts are charging.

Where to find markets/clients: First, you should let people know you're a ghostwriter. Mention it in your writer's bio, include it in your email signature, and make sure your website and social media sites like LinkedIn feature it as well.

Second, look for potential ghostwriting gigs on sites like FreelanceDaily.net, JournalismJobs.com, and even CraigsList.org. (I found two of my favorite clients on Craigslist!) Finally, if you write about a particular area, make sure that the people you come into contact with know you're a ghostwriter. I specialize in health, fitness, and nutrition, and many of my ghostwriting referrals come from people I've interviewed in the past. Usually a ghostwriting client is looking for a writer who already knows something about his subject matter, so play up your experience to your advantage.

How to break in: You need to have solid experience in whatever type of work you'll be ghosting. So if you write for a trade magazine, you can certainly ghost similar articles for a client. Same goes for ghosting books—you need to have published a book or two of your own first, so you can play up your experience to a potential client. If you're responding to a job post or a lead, you'll want to send a LOI detailing your relevant experience.

If you're ghostwriting books, be prepared for a lot of nonstarters, or writers who aren't serious about hiring a ghostwriter once they realize that they have to pay someone to write their book. On the other hand, there are clients out there, particularly those in business who want to write a book to enhance their credibility, and well-heeled clients who want to publish a family memoir, to keep you busy. (For the book-length guide to adding ghostwriting to your freelance repertoire, check out *Goodbye Byline, Hello Big Bucks: The Writer's Guide to Making Money Ghostwriting and Coauthoring Books*.)

Is That It?

And so we come to the end. I consciously chose to keep this book focused on one aspect of freelancing—writing nonfiction articles for print and online publications. You may find that writing articles is a great fit for you, or you may decide you want to branch out and try other types of writing work. Maybe your success in writing for money has encouraged you to tackle your first book.

The ever-changing freelance landscape means there are more opportunities than ever before for writers of all stripes, and that's good news for all of us. Stay open to possibilities, and to the fact that even when you plan something, your writing career may veer in a new and unexpected direction. That's part of the thrill—and satisfaction—when you choose to write for money.

A Note to Readers

First, I'd like to say thank you for buying this book! I truly appreciate my readers, and hope you've found everything you need to make the leap from unpublished to published and paid. Once you start writing for money, I think you'll be hooked and want to continue!

The freelance landscape is constantly changing, so please visit my blog, http://dollarsanddeadlines.blogspot.com, for the latest advice on writing for money. And if you have a quick question for me, shoot me an email at dollarsanddeadlines@gmail.com. I'm always happy to help my readers.

If you plan to pursue freelancing fulltime, I suggest my popular book, *Six-Figure Freelancing: The Writer's Guide to Making More Money*, which is aimed at more experienced writers who want to increase their income. If you're planning to expand into other types of writing work, and want to make more money (yes, I talk about making money a lot!), check out *Writer for Hire: 101 Secrets to Freelance Success*. They are both invaluable resources for writers with some experience. And if you plan on getting into ghostwriting, pick up *Goodbye Byline, Hello Big Bucks: The Writer's Guide to Making Money Ghostwriting and Coauthoring Books*.

Thank you again for buying this book, and I wish you all the best in your venture to write for money. I hope you'll find it as rewarding, and satisfying, as I have.

--Kelly James-Enger
dollarsanddeadlines@gmail.com

APPENDIX

Looking for more advice on writing for print and online markets? Here are some of my favorite resources:

Blogs

Some of my favorite blogs that cover freelancing for print and online markets include:

- All Freelance Writing, http://allfreelancewriting.com/blog;
- Dollars and Deadlines, http://dollarsanddeadlines.blogspot.com;
- Guerilla Freelancing, www.guerrillafreelancing.com;
- Make a Living Writing, www.makealivingwriting.com/;
- The Renegade Writer, www.therenegadewriter.com;
- The Urban Muse, www.urbanmusewriter.com; and
- WordCount--Freelancing in the Digital Age, http://michellerafter.com/.

Books/e-Books Available on Amazon/Kindle

13 Ways to Get the Writing Done Faster: 2 Pro Writers Share Their Secrets
Linda Formichelli and Carol Tice
E-book full of advice on working faster and making more money.

Full-Time Income in Part-Time Hours: 22 Secrets to Writing Success in Under 40 Hours a Week
Gretchen Roberts
If you're freelancing part-time, Gretchen Roberts' e-book gives plenty of strategies to help you maximize your time, leverage your earnings, and choose clients who pay well and respect your work.

Ready, Aim, Specialize! Create Your Own Writing Specialty and Make More Money!, second edition
Kelly James-Enger
One of my earlier books; it describes the ten hottest writing specialties and how to break into them as well as twenty actual queries that sold and hundreds of resources.

The Renegade Writer's Ultimate Guide to Marketing Your Freelance Writing: 27 Riffs from the Renegade Writer Blog on How to Earn More Money Doing What You Love

Linda Formichelli
E-book that includes smart advice from Linda Formichelli, coauthor of The Renegade Writer books/blog.

The Renegade Writer's Query Letters That Rock: The Freelance Writer's Guide to Selling More Work Faster
Linda Formichelli and Diana Burrell
E-book full of queries that worked, and why.

The Urban Muse Guide to Online Writing Markets
Susan Johnston
Susan Johnston's e-book shows you how to find online markets, track down editors, craft query e-mails that get noticed, and includes a directory of over fifty online writing markets that buy freelance articles.

Online Communities

- Cassell Network of Writers/Writers-Editors Network
  http://www.writers-editors.com
  Members have access to market info, publishing updates, and other information; basic membership $39/year ($29/year for online membership).
- Freelance Success
  www.freelancesuccess.com
  Includes a weekly e-mail newsletter with detailed market reports and access to an onsite bulletin board. $99/year.
- WorldwideFreelance.com
  http://www.worldwidefreelance.com/writing-markets
  For $24.95/year, you have access to a searchable database of 2,500 writing markets. This site also offers a free newsletter, free listing of 750 markets, and access to niche market lists for $6.95/list.

INDEX

24-hour rule 28, 33, 34
Anecdotal sources, see sources
Articles
    Examples 67-68, 73-74, 77-79, 82-84, 85-86, 93-98, 100-104, 105-116, 118-120, 127-131, 133-138, 140-141
    Types
        Features 88-120
        Profiles 121-131
        Q & A 80-87
        Quizzes 131-139
        Round-ups 139-143
        Shorts 60-68
ASJA (American Society of Journalists and Authors) 58
Assignments 54-55, 59-60
Bacon's Newspaper/Magazine Directory 18
"Back-up," see fact-checking
Blogs
    About freelancing 37
    Writing for 14-15
"Bongs," see rejections
Celebrities, locating and interviewing 122
Clips 10
Competing markets 29, 112
Consumer magazines, see markets
Contracts
    Examples 40, 153
    Negotiating changes 50-51, 163
    Specific provisions 40-49
Cooperation provisions (in contracts) 46
Contacting sources, see sources
Copyright 39-40
Cover letter 142, 152
Custom magazines, see markets
Debby Downer 32, 34
Deductions, see taxes
Dollars and Deadlines blog 8, 164
Essays, writing and selling 142-146
Exercise, importance of 35-36

Expenses (in contracts) 44-45
Expenses (business), see taxes
Fact-checking 79-80, 138-139
FOB, see front of book
Following up 27, 151-152
Freelance income, average 8-9
Friends (freelancing) 36-38
Front of book ("FOB") 15, 26, 60
Gale Directory of Publications and Broadcast Media 18
Getting paid, see payment issues
Ghostwriting 171-172
Goals, setting 29, 58
Guidelines, see writers' guidelines
Help a Reporter Out ("HARO") 99
Ideas, coming up with 11-13, 61, 98-99, 112
Income survey, annual 8-9
Income, freelance 8-9
Income, gross 8-9, 55
Income, net 55-56
Indemnification provisions (in contracts) 48-49
Interviews, see sources
Invoices 153-155
Killed, when an article is 161-162
Kill fees (in contracts) 45-46
Lead time 21
Letter of agreement 153-154
Letter of introduction ("LOI") 16, 20, 149-151
Markets
   Locating and identifying potential ones 13-18
   Online resources 14
   Types
     Blogs 14-15
     Consumer magazines 15-16
     Custom magazines 16
     Newspapers 17
     Online 13-14
     Print 15-17
     Trade magazines 16-17, 88-98
Nut graph/nut paragraph 83, 100, 101, 106, 117, 118
"On acceptance" (payment) 44
One-shots 13, 167
Online markets, see markets
"On publication" (payment) 44, 163
Payment issues 154-156, 163

Payment provisions, in contracts 44
"Pay-or-die" letter 155-156
Platform 166
PMA/Positive Mental Attitude 31-32
Profit motive 55-56, 58
Profiles, see articles
Q & A, see articles
Query/queries
   Examples 22-26, 62-63, 113-114, 148-149
   Format and purpose 21, 148-149
"Real people" sources, see sources
Regular clients 167-169
Reprints 166-167
Researching articles 59-62, 64-66, 69-70, 81, 88-89, 93, 99, 114, 122, 163
Reselling work, see reprints
Resubmissions/resubs 28
Rejection, coping with 28, 33-34
Resilience 33
Reslanting 28-29, 112-120
Ready, Aim, Specialize 11
Restrictive covenants (in contracts) 46-47
Rewriting 33, 54, 60, 79, 84, 162-163
Rights provisions (in contracts) 41-44
Sidebars 111
Six-Figure Freelancing 8, 52
SMART goals 29
Social media, using as a freelancer 30, 169
Sources
   Anecdotal ("real people") 116
   How many to use 93
   Interviewing 65-66, 70, 156-157
   Locating 64-65, 69-70, 159-160
   Recording 65-66, 70, 89
Specializing 165-166
Studies, locating 61-62
Standard Periodical Directory 16, 18
Subheads/subheadings 73, 93, 100, 105
Taxes
   Common questions about 57-58, 161
   Deductions, for freelancers 55-57
   Tax Guide for Small Business 57
"TEA" (Thank, Explain, Ask) 50, 53
Templates 147-158
Thank-you notes 66, 112, 157-158

Time peg 21
TK 163
Trade magazines, see markets
Uniquely qualified 12, 14, 15, 24, 62, 148, 160
Warranty provisions (in contracts) 47
Websites, see markets (online)
Word count 63, 67, 79, 118, 148-149, 167-168
Worst case scenario 32-33
Writers' guidelines 22
Writer's Market 10
Writing for businesses/corporations 170-171

email Kelly / dollars and deadlines@gmail.com
subject line: super awesome bonus
// dollarsanddeadlines.blogspot

<u>Medical</u>　　　　　　　　<u>Writing</u>
　　Breast cancer
　　Bipolar
　　Scolosis
　　Celiac

<u>Art</u>　　　　　　　　　Doc. in Car

Query

¶1 - lead/grabber
2 - why write it (why her readers should care)
3 - nuts + bolts
    interview
      title
       length
        where in publication
        sidebar
4. ISG

---

p27 Followup - 8 to 12 weeks
    email - give editor a deadline!

p37 Blogs for writers

p40 Contract
p153 Letter of Agreement

64 Sample: request for interview -
    Backgrounds: Wikipedia

67 FORMAT for Sending Article

79 Article FORMAT w/ fact-checking notes

112 Reslant

Sources

p. 61	database for 22m medical journal article
62	Science & Health – STANFORD
64-5 + 69	Sources for EXPERTS (question lost)
66	Headset & Recorders
~~11~~	ASJA – membership
14	online / Blogs
16-18	Directories
37	BLOGS (+ 15)
174	Blogs / books / on line source

Liz
1 832-279-3619

Published by My Improvise Press.com

CPSIA information can be obtained at www.ICGtesting.com
Printed in the USA
BVOW05s2043040815

411839BV00015B/107/P

9 780983 663362